DEFYING POVERTY
WITH BICYCLES

How to Succeed with Your Own
Social Bike Business Program

Sue Knaup

Publisher's Cataloging-in-Publication data
Knaup, Sue.
    Defying poverty with bicycles : how to succeed with your own
social bike business program / Sue Knaup.
    p. cm.
    ISBN 978-0-9859889-0-6
    Includes index and bibliographical references.
1.   Cycling. 2. Transportation --Social aspects. 3. Choice of
transportation --Social aspects. 4. Poverty. 5. Social action. 6. Social
change. 7. Social entrepreneurship. I. Title.

HM831 .K635 2012
303.48/4 --dc23   2012947166

Printed in the United States of America

First Edition

ISBN 978-0-9859889-0-6

One Street Press
P.O. Box 3309
Prescott, Arizona 86302
USA

www.onestreet.org

This book is dedicated to all the leaders with the courage and tenacity to launch their own Social Bike Business program.

iv

CONTENTS

PREFACE

About This Book

Consider this book your guide into an entrepreneurial journey. I hope it will open new concepts in business and reveal the valuable expertise of impoverished people, cracking open for-profit and nonprofit conventions to show you a new way to lend a hand to our struggling world.

My own journey toward these discoveries took a much longer route until I finally landed on the idea of One Street, a unique international bicycle advocacy nonprofit. Along with my founding board members, we launched our Social Bike Business program in 2007, our first year, because we recognized it as primary to our mission of increasing bicycling by helping local leaders. One Street is unique because we never take the spotlight away from local leaders. Their programs always remain their programs. We focus on increasing bicycling because bicycles are the canaries of healthy communities. Try this observation sometime. Wherever you see lots of bikes you'll always find healthier, happier people and thriving economies. But many people, even in communities with lots of bicycling, still do not benefit from bicycling.

In our first year, discussions with community leaders in the U.S., Eastern Europe and Africa often turned to the lack of affordable, durable transportation bicycles designed for people who live in poverty. To such people, a transportation bicycle can mean the difference between unemployment and a job because bicycling is six times faster than walking at their most common speeds—twelve miles per hour and two miles per hour respectively. Of primary importance to these leaders was that a bicycle dramatically extends the distance someone can travel for work without having to pay public transport fees that can add up to thousands of dollars in a year or car costs that easily top three thousand dollars each year. I captured the details of these discussions to fortify our Social Bike Business program and identify the problems it needed to solve.

The bike industry stopped making quality, affordable transportation bicycles a long time ago. What we have been left with are bicycles that meet only two of those three criteria—quality transportation bikes that cost several months' salary or garbage, bicycle-shaped-objects that breakdown after a few rides, if they are safe to ride at all.

I also heard repeatedly from local partners that even if impoverished people in their communities managed to obtain a quality transportation bicycle, there was no place for them to go to get the bike fixed. Owners of for-profit bike shops focus on selling fancy bicycles to advantaged people in order to meet their monetary bottom line. This means they must locate their stores in upper class neighborhoods and offer the top of the line products. Even their staff must be chosen and trained to focus on privileged customers. All of this adds up to a very unwelcoming environment for disadvantaged people and even some people who want to try bicycling for the first time.

In response, do-it-yourself volunteer-run bicycle co-ops and collectives have been popping up in cities across the U.S. and Europe. While the intention is good, the loose organization structure tends to form around the limited time these volunteers can offer. Open hours are often sporadic and unpredictable. Also, many of these programs are based on the do-it-yourself concept designed for people with time to spare. Unfortunately, most disadvantaged people cannot afford the time it takes to build a bike or learn bicycle repair by trial and error. Much of what these volunteer-run programs set out to accomplish aligns with Social Bike Business. If you have led such a program, but want to build a more sustainable business model, Social Bike Business might offer you some interesting ideas.

With for-profit bike shops serving privileged bicycle enthusiasts and volunteer-run co-ops and collectives serving people with time to spare, most distressed neighborhoods are still left without dependable bike shops that are designed to serve the needs of their residents. Anyone who has ever lived on the margins of their society or suffered the stress of poverty knows that impoverished people are not just monetarily poor. Low paying jobs far from home consume whole days with long work hours and grueling commutes. Childcare and assistance with basic chores are unobtainable luxuries. Even without a job, social service requirements present an endless maze that crushes the most inspired entrepreneurial spirit. In agricultural areas of the world, simply tending a small plot and caring for animals uses all the energy these food sources provide.

Because people who live in or even near poverty are so consumed by the daily stress of survival they cannot engage in society. This often means isolation from community activities and even well-meaning programs designed to serve them. Unfortunately, such charitable service programs neglect to actually engage the people they are meant to serve, the very people who understand the struggle and language of their neighbors.

The Social Bike Business program is designed to bridge all of these gaps by guiding struggling people toward their own entrepreneurial success. Advantaged people are well served by bike shops, collectives and co-ops. Now it's time to create the places that invite our most disadvantaged neighbors to purchase their own bike—refurbished or manufactured locally through the program—and engage in a new career that will enable them to lift themselves out of poverty. Even obtaining a quality transportation bicycle can save a person several hours each day if they had been walking and save them thousands of hard-earned dollars each year. Bicycles shrink cities at no charge. But this program does far more than that. It establishes bicycle community centers where struggling people can learn from each other about transportation bicycling and careers in bicycle business and beyond.

In the following chapters, you will learn how to plan for and launch your own Social Bike Business program, adapted to the needs and specialties of your particular community to ensure you reach your most disadvantaged neighbors. Your program can be as small as needed to succeed or as immense and complex as you believe you and your team can achieve. Think of this book as a menu to pick from rather than a prepared meal. Start where it makes sense for you and your team and go as far as you need to go. You might already have a small shop that would suffice as the main center for your program, so keep this in mind as you read about large centers designed for larger programs than yours needs to be. You and your team might want to focus on job training and refurbished used bikes. Then skip the chapter on bicycle manufacturing. This book is yours to do with what you like. Pull out the pieces that sing to you and shut the volume off on all the rest.

As you read, you will learn how to place the most disadvantaged people first and how to help them purchase their own bike through micro credit and subsidy qualification so they will value their bike. You will learn how to spot talents in people and offer a variety of career paths all based on bicycles, but designed to help them find work in many different fields, from business management to customer service to mechanics to owning their own business. You will learn proven business practices that ensure all employees of your program are paid a market rate salary. You will find ways to overcome the relentless stress and fear of poverty. And from this insight, you will learn how to choose the most effective means of reaching and engaging your community's most disadvantaged residents— their preferred way of communicating, the locations most inviting to them, what they need in order to attend a meeting or workshop including food and childcare, and many more vital details that are commonly forgotten in today's bicycle businesses and programs.

Be sure to study Chapter 1 because that is where you will have to be honest with yourself and your local leadership team. Are you envisioning a more casual and fun volunteer program that gives bikes away? A co-op or collective might be a better fit. Such programs can build the bike culture. You might also be a budding for-profit business owner. For-profit bike shops are necessary elements of every bicycling community and a very honorable path to take.

If you choose Social Bike Business, one important requirement is that you must live in the community and be prepared to help lead the organization that takes on the program. I have encountered several well meaning people who are enthusiastic about the program, but expect others to take it on without their assistance. They see its potential in another community or believe that an organization they do not lead should take it on. In fact, the only way for you to succeed with the program is to step into a leadership position and inspire others to join you in building this program so it serves the community where all of you live. No program can thrive if it is started or run by outsiders.

I understand that Social Bike Business is not for everyone. In order to succeed, each local program must compliment rather than compete with existing for-profit bike shops and co-ops/collectives. Each Social Bike Business program must fill an unfilled niche. That niche is service to and full engagement of the most disadvantaged people in each community. By filling that niche, Social Bike Business is designed to enable people to find their own path out of poverty through bicycles. According to the World Bank, eighty percent of the world's population is living in poverty. The Social Bike Business program opens a world of opportunities to them through bicycling. For this, they will continue to ride and perhaps even take up sport cycling. This will grow the whole bicycle movement and boost the bike industry as these formerly-poor join the advantaged bicycle enthusiasts of their community.

Social Bike Business is not about profits or charity. It is about helping people stand up against and defy poverty. Social Bike Business is about giving impoverished people the tools they need to leave poverty behind forever.

A Note on Terminology

Some readers may be disturbed by my use of terms such as "disadvantaged" and "impoverished" to describe the most important people to any Social Bike Business program. Others may not know what I mean by these terms. In the following chapters you will read more about finding and working with the people this program is designed to serve. Reaching them is critical, so you must investigate and learn about their struggles. Guidance for this investigative work requires the use of specific terminology. For now, keep in mind that this is not just about poverty. These are the people who have been shunned, oppressed, brutalized, marginalized, tormented, discarded, ignored, left out, abandoned, forgotten and isolated from the rest of their community. Poverty is a common result, but it is not the root cause. Finding any single term that captures such significance is not easy.

I have asked about proper terminology with the leaders of every serious partner organization I've worked with for this program. "Disadvantaged" has been the clear winner for over five years with "underserved" coming in a distant second. "Impoverished" seems to meet with the most approval when financial struggle is the core discussion point.

Please realize that my use of any of these terms is akin to VIP. No genuine Social Bike Business program can move ahead unless the most disadvantaged people in the community are considered the highest priority and welcomed as leaders of the program.

How One Street Helps Our Social Bike Business Partners

One Street's mission is to serve leaders of organizations who are working to increase bicycling. The word "serve" in our mission means that we never do the work of local leaders and we always ensure that they remain the face of bicycling in their communities. We help these local leaders build their organizations and plan for successful bicycle programs and campaigns, all the while respecting them as the experts on bicycling in their communities. Translating this to our Social Bike Business program means that your program remains your program—no contracts, no commitments, no required ties to One Street in order to receive our basic assistance.

You may wonder how we manage to do this. Our organization structure is modeled after other service organizations where those who fund the organization are not necessarily those who receive the services, though some still do contribute. We receive the majority of our funding from sponsors, foundations and individuals who believe in our work.

Our Social Bike Business program also falls under our overarching on-call service to any leader of any organization that is working to increase bicycling. Such leaders can call, email or Skype us anytime to ask for guidance with organization struggles, bicycle campaign ideas, brainstorming their next steps, and requests for the latest resources in bicycle advocacy and organization management. Any organization considering taking on Social Bike Business can contact us anytime for such basic assistance with no strings attached.

At a higher level, once the leaders of a locally-based organization decide to fully engage in the Social Bike Business program and require more commitment from us, we ask to be included in their major fundraising efforts for their program. Along with this, we add the program to our list of partners and connect them to our growing network so they can learn from others around the world. This helps us promote them as part of our international program including adding them to our Social Bike Business program web page and highlighting them during speaking engagements and in our international e-newsletter. This does not change our pledge to local ownership of the program. We always emphasize the local organization as the lead of each local program and never communicate directly to their members, partners or clients without their leaders present. While grantors and other major donors will see a line item for One Street's professional services in funding requests, the members, partners, customers and clients of the local program will only see the name of their organization as the entity responsible for the program.

Before being included in any fundraising effort, we work with the leaders of each local organization to agree on the level of effort they would like us to put into assisting with their plans. It could be as little as regularly scheduled conference calls with their staff and board members. In this case, our percentage of the funding requests would be very small. It could also be as significant as our committing to travel to their community for an extended stay to conduct organization planning and train-the-trainer workshops. In this case, One Street's time and travel costs could be a significant part of some funding requests. Most will fall between these two extremes. Regardless, all are based on the mutually agreed upon level of service the local organization requests from One Street.

At this higher level of assistance, we also pitch in to help with fundraising. This includes helping the leaders plan their program, research grants, find interested funders, take part in funder meetings with the local leaders, review drafts of grant proposals, and sometimes write and submit proposals to grantors more inclined to fund the local program through One Street e.g., U.S. foundations not equipped to fund overseas.

Whether or not these major fundraising efforts provide significant funding, One Street remains on-call to assist with all the smaller, basic steps necessary to help you and your fellow leaders reach your goals for your own Social Bike Business program. This includes achieving financial sustainability through income generation and freedom from dependence on significant grants and donations.

We also rely on the input of people like you in order to do a better job of serving local leaders around the world who are working to increase bicycling. This first edition only captures what we've learned to this point about the Social Bike Business program. We welcome your ideas for improvements and will recognize contributions we use in our acknowledgements section in future editions.

About the Author

Since the age of 12 (that's 36 years and counting) I've worked for and led nonprofit organizations in the fields of animal rights, environment, special populations and, for the past 16 years, bicycle advocacy at the local, national and international levels. Through these roles, I have discovered the astonishing impact anyone can make simply by valuing the expertise of those who are struggling. Rather than charity handouts, I learned that guiding struggling people into leadership positions can result in systemic changes for communities. From another angle, as the owner of a local bike shop for 13 years I gained invaluable insight, not only into the world of for-profit business, but the very heart of the bicycle industry.

In 2007, I founded One Street as an international service organization in honor of the many local organizations that are responsible for bringing bicycling back to communities, yet rarely get the credit. And through One Street's Social Bike Business program I've found the perfect balance of nonprofit compassion and business sustainability for helping impoverished people achieve their dreams with bicycles.

Most importantly, I'm thrilled to be writing this book. The Social Bike Business program is like a relief valve for me, releasing frustrations that have built up over decades of my previous experiences—nonprofits that forget our most disadvantaged neighbors, bikes for everyone else, fabulous innovations that fly right past the people who need them the most.

My hope is that this book will streamline a path to significant positive change for many aspiring leaders. This is not to knock the long, circuitous route. I certainly have learned a lot that way, but my guess is that a direct route will help you enjoy the fruits of your efforts much sooner.

Section
1

First
Steps

CHAPTER 1

Is Social Bike Business Right for You?

Before you decide whether Social Bike Business is right for you, you'll want to understand what social business is. Most importantly, social business serves social needs before profits. A genuine social business not only provides products and services that respond to the needs of disadvantaged people, but is also led or owned by disadvantaged people. Variations on this definition include nonprofit organizations that sell things to support their mission and for-profit companies that occasionally help disadvantaged people.

At One Street, we encourage our local Social Bike Business partners to strive for the genuine model, eventually. We understand however, that most local leaders are not living in poverty at the time they contact us for help. Starting an organization, especially one that will take on such a comprehensive program as Social Bike Business, requires free time and startup capital contributed by the founders, luxuries not often known to impoverished people. In Chapter 3 you'll read more about potential organization structures. For now, it's only important to envision how you and your team will strive toward a genuine social business model. Such a model will not just provide bikes and career training. It will also guide your most disadvantaged neighbors into jobs and leadership positions in your organization as it helps others launch their own Social Bike Businesses.

Social Business Origins and Current Trends

The term social business is often interchanged with social enterprise. While they aren't exactly the same, knowing these two terms are interchangeable will help you explore social business resources. Many of the best resources use the term social enterprise, so don't pass those up.

Social enterprise is usually used more as an umbrella term that captures nonprofits that sell things, for-profits that help people, and genuine social businesses that provide social products and services and are led by the peers of the people they serve.

While social business is a recent term, social enterprise goes back to the very first corporations, back to ancient Europe and India when companies were actually formed to serve social needs. That's mighty hard to believe these days! Unfortunately, even these very early corporations formed around a monetary bottom line, the idea that their main purpose was to make money. By the 16th century, lawmakers began to rein in corporate abuses. The Charitable Uses Act of 1601 England was passed to distance the truly charitable companies from those focused entirely on profits. I have found this act at the core of all the nonprofit legal structures I have encountered in countries around the world. But as its title suggests, it only serves organizations focused on charity—giving away goods and services. With for-profit corporations spun off as purely for profit and nonprofits deemed charities, nearly four hundred years passed with little expectation for business expertise to be used to solve social problems.

The earliest deliberate attempts at social enterprise are found in for-profit corporations of the 1800s when companies tested employee-owned co-op structures. We still see some of these today, but the structure has proven fragile, so very few remain. It wasn't until the 1970s when two very new concepts took hold that social enterprise as we know it today finally gained momentum. During that decade, micro lending organizations grew out of the idea of lending small amounts to entrepreneurial minded poor people to help them start their own business.

At the same time, community development corporations (CDC) took the stage in the United States as a means of organizing the residents of distressed neighborhoods along with significant funding from private and government investors to redevelop several blocks at once. The CDC movement has gained impressive momentum, resulting in resident-led redevelopments that serve their housing, schooling and recreational needs as they prevent the social harm of displacement and gentrification. While most CDCs are formed under a nonprofit structure, they represent some of the most successful social enterprises in existence today, some handling millions of dollars in development transactions each year. Their employees are neighborhood residents who receive market salaries and their products—new housing, businesses, schools and parks—all serve the needs of the disadvantaged residents of their neighborhood.

In recent years, as charitable contributions and government funding to nonprofits has steadily diminished, more and more nonprofits are looking to the social enterprise model for sustainable income generation. If you are the leader of a nonprofit experiencing similar stress, Social Bike Business could be your entry into this new way of generating income for your organization.

Muhammad Yunus, founder of Grameen Bank in Bangladesh,

was the first to use the term social business as a more credible form of social enterprise. Through his work with Grameen Bank and guiding impoverished people into business ownership, he discovered that a business focused on serving social needs could earn sufficient profits through implementing two key purposes at the same time: 1) providing products and services that serve the needs of impoverished people, 2) providing jobs and careers to those same people. He details this concept in his 2007 book *Creating a World Without Poverty*. One Street's Social Bike Business program strives toward this double purpose social business model: 1) providing the transportation bicycles as well as the repair and job training services impoverished people need, 2) hiring impoverished people as employees of the program and supporting others as they build new careers.

As the terms social enterprise and social business have gained popularity, so has the abuse of these terms. Major corporations have been under greater scrutiny lately and often attempt to hide behind these terms to present an altruistic image. Just as many corporations have employed "green washing" to create an illusion of environmental stewardship as they continue to devour natural resources, some are learning to use "social washing" to combat claims against the social harm they are causing worldwide. So, as you do further research on these concepts, keep a wary eye out for false models. As long as a company or corporation prioritizes a monetary bottom line, social needs will always fall by the wayside.

This explains why One Street does not use the term "triple bottom line" i.e., monetary-environmental-social. I have found that many companies and corporations that tout a triple bottom line fall short of carrying it through. The monetary bottom line often overrides the other two as companies under pressure to make the most profit seek out the most desperate, impoverished people to make their products, force them to work long hours and pay them the very least they will accept, thus heightening their poverty. The pressure to meet the monetary bottom line also tempts outsourcing to new, more desperate countries leaving a wake of laid-off employees behind. On the environmental side, practices that truly protect the environment, such as replanting trees and reclaiming waste are always more expensive than environmentally destructive practices. With a monetary bottom line included, many companies can only give lip service to the other two.

Instead, One Street's Social Bike Business model focuses on the social bottom line: the number of disadvantaged people served by the program. By following proven and successful business practices to increase the number of disadvantaged people served, the monetary and environmental bottom lines become unavoidable. In order to serve as many disadvantaged people as possible, the business must have strong and reliable profits. And because harming the environment harms people, this would subtract from the number of disadvantaged people served, so environmental stewardship becomes mandatory to achieve the bottom line.

Find our recommended social business resources in the Resources section, in particular: Grameen, Social Enterprise Toolbelt and NESsT.

What is Social Bike Business?

One Street's Social Bike Business program works with local leaders who are committed to providing disadvantaged people with affordable, quality transportation bicycles—refurbished and even manufactured locally through the program—and job training that opens their path out of poverty. Each local program, led by residents of the community, must envision providing these bikes and career training services at a comprehensive bicycle community center that will be the central location of their program. This center must be located in a place that welcomes the most disadvantaged residents of the community. It must be open at least five days a week during normal business hours. Ideally it will be large enough to accommodate a welcome area, bicycle sales and service, safe riding instruction, classrooms for job training, and eventually bicycle manufacture. The founders of the program must prioritize serving disadvantaged people before all others, even though everyone in the community should feel welcome. This means seeking out disadvantaged people from the very start and learning from them their bicycling and job training needs: what sort of bikes and equipment they need (to carry loads, to carry children, skinny tires for speed, fat tires for rough terrain, long wheelbase for extreme loads, short enough wheelbase for bus racks, etc.), the best times for meetings, what they need in order to attend meetings and workshops (food, childcare, etc.), and how they prefer to communicate (don't assume email or Facebook will work).

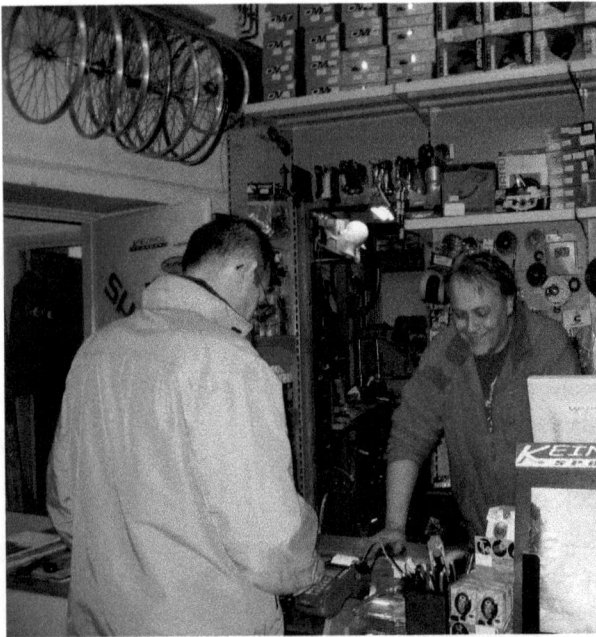

The founders must also be committed to making a profit from selling bikes, parts and services in order to grow the program, pay market wages, and serve as many disadvantaged people as possible. This means welcoming retail customers and charging full retail prices for everyone. In order to do this while still primarily serving impoverished people, the founders must commit significant time to creating a micro lending and subsidy program that allows these qualified individuals to purchase bikes, parts and services at full retail. Micro lending allows payment for the product or service over many months. Subsidies from grants and donations contribute to the purchase for the most disadvantaged customers. This system must include a multi-tiered requirement for proving their need including government social service records and neighborhood champions who can vouch for them. Read more details on this system in Chapter 7.

The founders must also envision hiring disadvantaged people into leadership positions and potentially even relinquishing their own leadership positions to disadvantaged people trained through the program. Read how One Street offers guidance on all of this in the Preface.

Keep in mind that your program will have its own unique shape and may not include all the possible elements found in this book. In order for your program to be considered a Social Bike Business program, you simply have to focus on providing bikes, career training and jobs to the most disadvantaged people in your community within a sustainable business model.

What is *Not* Social Bike Business?

As you consider the above concepts and whether they fit your vision for your new endeavor, you should also look at what is *not* Social Bike Business. The most common misconception I run into is volunteer-run programs and organizations. I hear this especially in the U.S. and Europe where volunteer-run bicycle co-ops and collectives are common. As you read in the Preface, most of these do not qualify as Social Bike Businesses, not only because they don't meet the requirement of market wages for employees, but because the majority of clientele they attract are advantaged, not disadvantaged. I realize that most Social Bike Business programs must initially be led by volunteers. The difference is that Social Bike Business programs are designed to bring in profits and pay all employees market wages as quickly as possible. Volunteer-run programs never have this aim.

This is closely followed by well-intentioned bicycle programs that forget one of the most important elements of a Social Bike Business program: that it must welcome the most disadvantaged people of the community. Common mistakes include choosing a location that is not welcoming or convenient to disadvantaged people. Others can be more subtle, including choosing a groovy name that appeals to advantaged young people but sends a signal to disadvantaged people that they are not the priority for the program.

I also often hear from eager new leaders wanting to launch a bicycle program for disadvantaged people, but with sport bicycles. Such recreational programs and bike clubs are important to bringing impoverished people into the bike culture of any community, just as for-profit bike shops and volunteer-run co-ops/collectives play an important role in building the bike culture. But they are also not Social Bike Businesses because they don't start with the priority needs of disadvantaged people: affordable transportation and careers out of poverty. However, such sport-focused program elements could be added to a well established Social Bike Business program once it is fully serving the bicycle transportation and job training needs of the majority of the disadvantaged people in the community.

There are also many other secondary program elements and income generators that can be added to established Social Bike Business programs such as public art from broken bike parts, bicycle machines, cargo bikes and bike rentals. But none of these should be mistaken for the primary elements of quality transportation bikes and career training. See Chapter 12 for details and other ideas for adding creative program elements once your program is established.

Is Social Bike Business Right for You?

Now you should be ready to take this short quiz to find out if Social Bike Business is the right direction for you.

YES   NO

☐   ☐   Do you and your team have the time and financial stability to invest in founding your organization and launching this program over the next few years?

☐   ☐   Do you and your team prioritize career development for the most disadvantaged people in your community?

☐   ☐   Can you and your team commit to serving the bicycle needs of disadvantaged people instead of only focusing on profits?

☐   ☐   Are you and your team passionate enough about serving the transportation needs of poor people that you can leave sport bicycling out of the program?

☐   ☐   Are you and your team eager to sell bicycles, parts and services at full retail prices in order to generate profits that will provide market wages and grow the program?

☐   ☐   Are you and your team committed enough to the program to establish a comprehensive bicycle community center in a distressed neighborhood?

☐   ☐   Can you and your team invest the time necessary to create a system for micro lending, raising funds to subsidize qualified individuals, and determining their qualification?

☐   ☐   Could you and others on your team hire disadvantaged people as employees and eventually move them into leadership roles in your organization?

If you answered "no" to any of the above, Social Bike Business is likely not the right direction for you at this time. This doesn't mean it never will be. If you believe you and your team can overcome these concerns, use this manual and contact us for ideas to change your answers to "yes." If you can already answer "yes" to all, you should definitely read on to learn how you can launch your own Social Bike Business program.

CHAPTER 2

Assembling Your Team & Crafting Your Mission

Finding the best people for your leadership team is the most important early step you must take as a founder of your organization and Social Bike Business program. You cannot do it alone. Some people try, but these independent individuals usually find that starting their own for-profit bike shop or consulting business better suits their needs. In order to create the very best organization and program that truly serves the needs of your community's most disadvantaged people you must assemble a strong leadership team. At One Street, we've found that between five and 12 is the best number of leaders because with fewer than five you won't have enough hearts and minds to come up with the best ideas and with more than 12 either chaos or apathy ensues.

Most Social Bike Business programs will start in the nonprofit structure, so I will refer to this founding leadership team as your board of directors. See the next chapter for details on other potential organization structures. Boards of directors of nonprofits are expected to be volunteers because nonprofits are seen as charities, selflessly serving social needs. This is a good thing in some respects because voluntary boards of directors avoid conflicts of interest when discussing various ways of bringing income to the organization. It can also be a bad thing because voluntary board members often see their duties as low priority since they are not getting paid.

Recently, the practice of making the top employee, often called the executive director, a voting member of the board of directors has been gaining popularity with nonprofits. This ensures continuity between the paid staff and volunteer board members and prevents the demeaning of the executive by board members that often results from the old nonprofit practice of complete separation and board dominance. The end result is much more of a team spirit and aligns with common practice in for-profit corporations. Consider this as you look for your fellow founding leaders as well as which role on this leadership team you would prefer.

Before seeking your fellow founders and leaders, you must first understand that the vast majority of people are not leaders. Leaders are very strange people who love to attend meetings, study budgets, envision a program years from the present time, and see the whole organization all at once. Most people hate this sort of thing and would much prefer hands-on work that shows results right away. These folks can be your volunteers and later your staff members, your helpers for daily tasks and big jobs that require lots of hands. However, never try to force a hands-on helper into serving on your board of directors or taking a job in management for your program.

Another group you never want to invite into a leadership role are your experts. These are the accountants, attorneys, public officials, master mechanics, engineers, graphic designers, computer whizzes and others who offer to help your program. Very rarely, you might run into a dual personality sort who is an expert but also loves leadership duties. However, most experts prefer to focus on their expertise. *Never* torture these wonderful experts by coercing them onto your board of directors to sit through meetings and sift through reports. You need to keep them happily engaged in activities that fit their passion. Keep their contact info handy for when you need their particular talents.

Regarding contact info, this is one of the most important systems you will set up for your organization. Create this system right away, because you will likely speak with many, many people before you finally find your other founding leaders. Don't let any of these people slip through the cracks. Even though most are not going to become leaders, each and every one of them has the potential for becoming active volunteers, future staff members, experts, donors and those all-important networkers who tell everyone they know about your organization.

There are lots of fancy software programs available for keeping track of supporters of your organization. But if you're on a tight budget, as most new organizations are, a spreadsheet such as Excel will do a fine job. Make sure to create separate columns for first and last name and each section of the mailing address. This allows you to transfer the spreadsheet file into a label-making file for mailings. Also include a column for email. You can actually copy a whole column of emails directly into an email send-to field and, if it comes from Excel, the email program will automatically add the needed semi colons separating each address. Very handy for communicating with these folks and keeping them excited about your work. When you send mass emails, always hide addresses by using BCC or a list service and include instructions on how recipients can unsubscribe from future emails in case they are not interested. Also include in your spreadsheet a column for contributions and another next to it for the date of contribution. This will give you a gauge for when to ask for an annual renewal of their support. And don't forget to add a column where you can note their particular talents whether as a potential leader, expert, or volunteer. This will allow you to sort the list using this column so you can easily find the type of helpers you're looking for at any given time.

I'm sure that sorting people better suited as volunteers and experts narrows your list of potential founding leaders significantly. That's a good thing. Look for that passion for oversight and governance. Ask your potential candidates if they would be happy attending monthly meetings. Look for people with previous experience serving on boards of directors. If they want to do it again, that's a sure sign they are leadership material. And make sure they are people you know and trust.

One important warning at this point is that self-serving people with their own personal agendas often latch onto new organizations as a lazy way for them to achieve their personal goals. New organizations appear vulnerable and offer them a way of pushing their agenda without having to bother with all the work of founding their own organization. This may sound like a plot from Hollywood, but I'm afraid it is all too common. Sometimes such people are difficult to distinguish from true leaders who are genuinely eager to help build the organization you describe to them. Make sure all of your trusted fellow leaders are attuned to this threat in order to avoid inviting such individuals to serve on the board. In case one slips through, early board tasks can help reveal inappropriate board members as well as bring your leadership team closer together because they will require you to work as a team toward a common goal. People with personal agendas will not put up with these processes. Working together to accomplish these early tasks can also reveal those who may be potential future leaders, but are not ready yet. This can give you and the others a respectful way of asking these inappropriate people to step down from their leadership role that they will actually appreciate.

Once you have a strong leadership team together, it's time to get to work building a great organization that will serve your community for many generations. Your two most important early tasks as the founding leaders are:

1. Writing and approving your organization's mission statement
2. Naming your organization

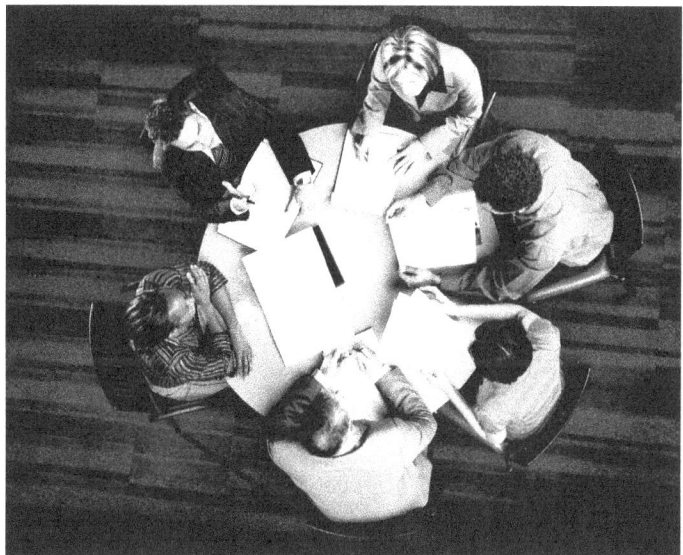

Mission Statement

Consider the mission statement of your organization as its guide far into the future after you have stepped out of your leadership role. In *one sentence*, it must clearly state your organization's unique purpose, distinguish it from other nearby organizations, and show who it is meant to serve and where that service will take place. It will become the all important filter for you and your fellow leaders as new ideas are brought to you. It will also keep future leaders on the same path you and your team intended for the organization. If your mission is to serve the bicycling needs of disadvantaged people in your community and a well-meaning funder offers you a grant to add a swimming pool to your bicycle community center, you and your fellow leaders will have no problem respectfully turning down that grant. But let's say your mission statement was as unclear and hollow as many institutional and governmental program missions. It might go on for several verbose sentences or even keep to one like: Creating a better community. In that case, you and your fellow leaders would have a very hard time explaining to this kindhearted funder why a swimming pool does not fit with your organization.

Another important point regarding your mission statement, particularly in regard to Social Bike Business, is that in order for your nonprofit to sell products and services without having to pay income tax on that income (one of the main benefits of using a nonprofit structure), those products and services must be directly connected to your organization's mission statement. When you incorporate your organization as a nonprofit, you will submit a document to your government that describes your organization's purpose and operations. In the U.S., this document is called the organization's "Articles of Incorporation." In other countries it may be called the "constitution," "articles of association," "statutes" or similar. No matter what it is called, it will include your mission statement as the organization's purpose.

When your Social Bike Business program is up and running and you begin bringing in money from selling products and services, attentive government officials will want to know how these sales are supporting your nonprofit mission. Sometimes even nasty bystanders who just want to make trouble for your organization will ask to see your financial statements, which are public records, and they can sound alarms if sales income has no connection to the mission. In the U.S., if your mission statement does not clearly support the sales of bicycles and job training services, you will have to pay income tax on that income. Note that I am only referring to income tax here. You may still need to collect sales tax from your customers for the products you sell (not services) and deliver that sales tax to your local government. Read more about this in Chapter 9. Other countries have similar and sometimes stricter laws to restrict income generation to a nonprofit's tax exempt purpose, i.e., its mission statement.

Understanding the difference between vague and specific mission statements also helps here. If your organization's mission is to serve the bicycling needs of disadvantaged people in your community, selling transportation bicycles and job training services fits perfectly. However, if your mission is to create a better community, you and your fellow leaders might have to waste a lot of time explaining to officials why selling bicycles and job training services is important to your mission. Keep this in mind as you and your fellow leaders work on your mission statement.

One distinction you'll want to keep in mind is the difference between a mission statement and a tagline. Your mission statement must do a lot of work—capture the purpose of the organization, clearly state where it works and who it serves, and act as an effective filter to avoid distractions. A tagline doesn't have all that responsibility. A tagline is simply a catchy line that captures the essence of your mission and can be useful in marketing and promotions.

Naming Your Organization

After you are all happy with your mission statement, your next very important task is to come up with the perfect name for your organization. Deciding on a name is one of the most enjoyable activities a founding group of leaders gets to do, so enhance this fun by choosing a relaxing time and place for this special meeting.

The name must capture the mission of the organization as it captures the imagination of anyone who hears it. Just as with your mission statement, avoid vague, institutional, boring language. The name of your organization will be the first thing people will encounter. Make it eye catching, intriguing, and welcoming to impoverished people, and, most importantly, memorable. The world doesn't need any more organizations with names like: The Association of Coalitions or The Institute of Bureaus for the Alliance of Institutes. Ask yourselves what is exciting about your community, what's exciting about providing bicycles to the people who need them the most, and what has excited each of you about this great new organization you're founding together. Use lots of paper, maybe a whole wall to write out all of these ideas. Then stand back and look at all those long descriptions and start circling the words that jump out at all of you. Somewhere in that excited mess of inspiration will lie the perfect name for your organization, a name you and all the people who take part will be proud to display and promote. Also be sure that the name you choose is not at all similar to other organizations that serve your area. Search the internet, check the local phone directory and look at lists of organizations in your area. This will avoid confusing your potential clients, helpers and funders as well as angering the other organization's leaders.

Another possibility is that your Social Bike Business program is only one of many programs offered by your organization. In this case, you can give it its own program name. Even as a program, you and your team will still have to take into account all of the above concerns.

Logo

One more fun project you and your team will have to tackle soon after you complete your mission statement and choose a great name, is the creation of your organization's logo (unless you are working through an established organization that already has a logo). This isn't as urgent as completing your mission and choosing a name, but you will soon find a need for it. In Chapter 4, I note the necessity of a website and your organization's website must include its logo.

Creating a logo is another excuse for a fun meeting. Ask all the leaders to bring design elements and colors they think capture your organization. Include elements from your community and culture. Steer away from bureaucratic symbols and shapes that look like existing organizations in your area. Make your logo unique, simple and a shape that everyone will recognize from far away.

Sometimes this process of finding founding leaders and establishing the mission and name of the organization gets all mixed up. In fact, mixing it all up might be the best way to go about it. Even if you are the brain child, the original founder, consider how you would attract other founders. You'd have to tell them something about the organization you envision to ensure they are just as passionate as you are to see it succeed. These early discussion points can be critical seeds that lead to the final mission statement and name. But be careful not to mistake them for your actual mission statement. Remember my point earlier that it takes at least five dedicated leaders to come up with the best ideas. This also applies to the final mission statement for your organization. Only with five or more hearts and minds deeply engaged in discussing what this organization could accomplish, will the best mission statement and name emerge.

Involving Disadvantaged People from the Start

I mentioned in Chapter 1 that it is most likely that you and your fellow founding leaders are not disadvantaged. This is because people who live in or near poverty simply do not have the time or resources required to invest in founding an organization. But there are always exceptions to this rule. If your community has even one impoverished resident with the talents and qualities of a leader who is willing to give significant time to helping found your organization, consider yourselves extremely lucky. To have someone so expert on the needs of poor people on your founding board will ensure your team finds the most effective path toward succeeding with your Social Bike Business program.

In order to give yourselves the best chance of finding such a person, you've got to first learn how to connect with people living in distressed areas of your community. Is there a well respected community center, church or other meeting place in the neighborhood? If so, go there and ask the staff and regulars if they know of anyone interested in helping found your organization. Describe the leadership role you're looking for, but also take note of experts and volunteers who step forward. Add them to that contacts list I mentioned earlier. You may also know social workers, bus drivers or school teachers who work in distressed neighborhoods in your community. Ask them if any residents of these neighborhoods have caught their eye as having leadership talents.

If you are lucky enough to find willing leaders from these neighborhoods, realize that your chosen meeting times and locations as well as your chosen communications methods become all the more important. No matter who serves on your leadership team, these choices are always important in order to ensure all can attend. But when you engage impoverished people in leadership roles, you must become hypersensitive to their needs if you expect them to continue on your team. This will make all of you better, more compassionate leaders in general.

Choose a time that allows them to return from a job that likely goes well past five o'clock. Realize that weekends are likely the only quality time they can spend with their families. If you can find a place that's kid friendly, this could help them provide time to both your organization and their children. Avoid meeting in restaurants because this sets them up for either paying far more than they can afford for food or awkwardly having to refuse to order even as everyone else does. Choose a location near their neighborhood so they don't have to spend money on public transport. And always provide childcare and plenty of food to take care of the most likely reasons that would prevent them from attending.

Once they are on board, choose a communication system that easily works for them. If they have no easy access to a computer, designate another leader responsible for going to their house or telephoning them with updates and delivering meeting materials within the same timeframe that all the others receive them.

Conducting Productive Meetings

Understanding how to conduct productive meetings is important throughout the life of any organization. But it is vital at the start, otherwise the organization might never get started.

The first step happens at least five days before the meeting. You or another leader must send a *draft* agenda to all the other leaders and ask for their input. Designate a deadline at least two days prior to the meeting when agenda changes and new agenda items must be proposed to the leader who sent out the draft. If these are simple changes and additions, this leader can go ahead and make them. However, if they are significant, this two day window allows them to send around a revised draft for comments and input. Another very important role of this deadline for agenda changes is that it prevents chaos during the meeting caused by random topics brought forward to discuss. By having a clear and agreed upon system for changing the agenda well before the meeting, all leaders will be comfortable sticking to the agenda, which will result in completion of all discussions and adjourning on time.

This leads into the next important step: starting your initial meetings by agreeing on meeting rules. Start with a blank flip chart or white board and ask the others for suggested rules that will ensure you all reach your intended meeting goals. This gives each leader a chance to offer rules that will prevent behaviors that have disturbed them in other meetings they've attended. Common meeting rules include:

- Only one person speaks at a time.
- Each agenda item must end with a decided action and a person responsible for completing it.
- All cell phones must be turned off.
- A time keeper is designated to ensure the meeting finishes on time.
- And so on...

This process of listing rules should take no more than five minutes. You can then post the list in easy sight of all attendees in case the meeting starts to spin out of control and use it to remind people of the agreed upon rules. After starting a few meetings with this listing of meeting rules, you can designate the favorites as your agreed upon meeting rules for all future meetings.

The last recommendation I would like to offer here is to assign a note taker at the very start of each meeting. Leadership meetings can cover lots of territory very quickly and unless someone is taking notes, great ideas will be lost. Not only are such losses a shame for the organization, they can also create resentment in the leaders who offered the ideas and then discover they have been ignored. Usually the loss of great ideas is not intentional, but to a budding leader, it can appear that the others regard their ideas as less important than their own. Avoid this potential rupture in your team by designating a note taker who can capture everyone's ideas, spell out the decided actions and set the names of those responsible next to each action item.

After the meeting, make sure that this note taker sends them around as a draft for everyone to review to ensure there are no omissions. At the next meeting, include an early agenda item for all of you to approve these notes at which point they will become the official minutes for your files. Keeping track of meeting minutes will give all of you a clear record of when decisions were made. And once your organization becomes well known in your community, they will also serve as important records of your professional conduct in case anyone questions your activities.

Read on to learn more about creating strong organization structures that will give your program goals the framework needed to serve impoverished people with bicycles.

CHAPTER 3

Choosing Your Organization's Structure

There are really only three options for organization structures available to leaders seeking to launch their own Social Bike Business program:

1. For-profit
2. Hybrid
3. Nonprofit

Below, I will summarize each, ending with nonprofit because that is the structure that we recommend. Make sure to read each and if one of the others seems like a better fit, do further research to ensure it is your best choice before making the leap. I will spend the rest of this chapter on the details of using the nonprofit structure to serve your Social Bike Business program.

For-profit Structure

The upside of going with the for-profit structure is that you will have to follow proven profit making practices. This can be a mindbender for those used to the nonprofit world. But even this will get you into trouble with the Social Bike Business program because the easiest way to make profits is to sell products with the highest profit margins (high-end, expensive racing bicycles and parts) to the most affluent people and be located in a place that attracts these people. While you can try to bridge the gap between serving advantaged and disadvantaged people, that monetary bottom line will continually force you to make decisions based on profits rather than serving the needs of disadvantaged people.

A for-profit structure could certainly work for a scaled down version of a Social Bike Business program, but you will have to battle the assumed monetary bottom line for the life of the organization. At least this structure is well-known and there are mechanisms for raising startup capital. However, these are always in the form of investment loans that must be paid back along with a hefty interest payment. Grants and donations are not an option for small for-profit businesses.

The for-profit model will be especially enticing to lone leaders who are not interested in working with a leadership team. While there are several ways to incorporate as a for-profit business (C and S corporations in the U.S.), most small business owners avoid incorporation, at least in their first ten years of operation. Full incorporation brings some liability protection to the company's owners, but it also shifts ownership from the founder as a single person, to a board of directors and any other investors in the company. This complex structure consumes vast amounts of energy in meetings and communications with this ownership group and loses the agility of a single person owner.

Unlike the corporate structure of a nonprofit organization, for-profit corporations must focus entirely on making profits and prove this single-minded effort to their board and investors. As you'll read later in this chapter, working with and communicating with a nonprofit board of directors directly serves the mission of the organization because these people are there to assist with that mission. In contrast, a for-profit's board of directors and its investors do not need to care how the profits are obtained as long as no laws are broken. This backdrop makes for far less inspiring interactions.

Simpler options in the U.S. are the Limited Liability Company (LLC) and a Partnership, both offering some liability protection but avoiding the complexity of full corporation. However, most for-profit business owners in countries around the world choose the simplest business structure, commonly known as "sole proprietor" status. This means the business is not incorporated and thus the owner is the responsible entity. While sole proprietorship lacks the broad protection of incorporation, at least in the U.S. it comes with basic protections, which should suffice as long as you do your bookkeeping and do your best to keep your customers and employees out of danger. Because the owner takes all the responsibility, sole proprietorship avoids the complications of incorporating, including having to assemble a board of directors.

Unfortunately, such an individual leadership structure will repel anyone who may have considered helping and prevent the broad community involvement that a nonprofit entices. Because of this, a sole proprietor-run Social Bike Business will likely not extend past a bike shop framework. But this is in fact one of the ultimate goals of the program— social bike shops owned and run by graduates of the job training part of the program. So there's certainly no reason that a lone leader shouldn't simply start there, except that you will not enjoy the benefits provided to these social bike shops by the program. Just keep in mind that by choosing the for-profit structure you will limit its program capacity to a basic bike shop and, in order to serve the needs of disadvantaged people you will have to rein in the temptation to sacrifice your goals in order to make more profits from wealthy people.

You can find links to more information on starting a for-profit social bike shop in the Resources section. Also check into the U.S. IRS Business Structures web page, National Bicycle Dealers Association, the U.S. Small Business Administration, the European Small Business Alliance, your own Chamber of Commerce, local small business associations, and your local colleges and universities.

Hybrid Structure

The hybrid option is slowly coming online. These hybrid companies are forming in various parts of the world in an attempt to create a corporate structure that caters to the needs of social businesses. A hybrid corporation's legal status is closer to a for-profit's and encourages social outcomes over profits. Unfortunately, the policy language that guides them is focused entirely on the handling of investments and preventing lawsuits from investors and shareholders if decisions are made for the public good rather than maximizing profits. Investors often only receive their principle investment back without interest, allowing all profits to go toward the social purpose. The rest of the required structure resembles a for-profit corporation or Limited Liability Company (LLC). Interest-free investments and freedom to make socially beneficial decisions within a publicly traded for-profit corporation might be attractive for some leaders looking to launch a massive Social Bike Business program. However, we have not yet encountered an organization with ambitions to trade on Wall Street or the luxury of working with investors. Without these, the benefits of a hybrid are moot.

The main downside of choosing a hybrid structure instead of a nonprofit structure is the same as a for-profit structure—no donations or grants. Most people will have no idea what it is, making your organization look suspicious at first glance. Potential donors will steer clear because it appears to be for-profit and does not allow tax deduction of their donation. Even retail customers will be suspicious of the organization's social claims because its structure will be similar to a for-profit company. Foundations and other investors can invest in a hybrid, but that hybrid must return the principle investment in a given amount of time. A hybrid does not qualify for foundation grants.

In the U.S. two new hybrid structures, benefit corporations and L3Cs, are gaining some popularity. The benefit corporation structure protects the corporation from investor and shareholder lawsuits if decisions are made for social benefits instead of maximizing profits. Otherwise it's basically the same as a conventional for-profit corporation.

L3C is the other new hybrid structure. It stands for Low-profit Limited Liability Company. As you can see from its name, it's not much different from the for-profit Limited Liability Company (LLC) structure. In fact, the filing paperwork is virtually the same as a for-profit LLC. Vermont was the first state to pass legislation recognizing L3C companies in 2007 and has since passed benefit corporation legislation. As of 2012, a dozen or so states have either passed or are considering passing legislation that recognizes these sorts of corporations and companies.

A somewhat telling sign that the L3C structure might not be the sweeping answer some thought it might be is that the website of the main organization supporting L3Cs, Americans for Community Development, has sat all but empty for four years as of this writing. Benefit corporations also have a support organization called B Lab that also offers certifications to conventional for-profit corporations called B Corporation Certification. Their website is a bit more up-to-date, but speaks entirely to investor-based and publicly traded corporations.

All in all, this paints a long road ahead for hybrids, but, as with many innovations, there may be a hybrid structure that is yet to be invented that will revolutionize the way we form socially minded organizations. Until then, I recommend that you stay with proven structures. So, onto nonprofit.

Nonprofit Structure

As I mentioned earlier, the nonprofit structure is the most common and most likely to succeed for the Social Bike Business program. This is because it is commonly understood by all concerned parties—officials, funders, customers, clients and leaders of the organization. It is also the only type of organization structure that can legally offer tax deductions on donations, which makes it the only structure that can seek significant grants. While grants can be difficult to obtain, especially for a new organization, and are rarely repeated, securing significant grants early on can launch a Social Bike Business program from plan directly into income generation. Such grants and large donations can cover the startup capital you need to build or renovate your program's bicycle community center, stock it with its first inventory and supply it with all the classroom supplies necessary for organizing your first Social Bike Business career training courses. And unlike for-profit capital investments, nonprofit grants and donations do not have to be returned.

The downside of choosing a nonprofit structure is that you will inherit that four hundred year old assumption that nonprofits are charities run by volunteers that give things away to poor people. If you and your team can consciously counter this pervasive stereotype and ensure that all new leaders and helpers understand that your organization does not fit into this unsustainable mold, you will succeed. But realize that combating that stereotype is far more difficult than you might assume. Funders and donors will scoff at their donations being used for "overhead," i.e., paying your employees market wages, paying for construction and utility bills, keeping your center clean and welcoming, and investing in proper equipment so everyone can do a great job. Too many donors and foundations still believe that the only place their money should go is into temporary emergency items for the poor. This is why you will want to wean your organization off of a dependence on grants and donations and start bringing in income from sales and services as soon as possible.

But at the start, when grants and donations will be necessary, you and your team will have to learn how to quickly articulate this new paradigm. You'll have to describe to potential donors what social business means and that the best place for their donations and grants to go is into salaries and infrastructure that will enable impoverished people to break free of the charity cycle.

Another danger will follow once you secure a few grants. There's nothing like receiving a big check that can be spent immediately on program needs. So, when it's time to shift energy into income generating practices, some on your team will have a hard time making the shift. They'll argue for investing the majority of time on grant writing and research, that the countless hours sending off proposals are worth it because the next one might just be awarded. Remind these starry eyed leaders that on average just ten percent of all grant proposals are awarded; that each proposal can add up to a full week of full-time labor when you include research, writing the proposal to fit the funder's specific needs, and finally delivering the proposal exactly as the funder expects. If you and your team must write ten proposals in order to receive one, remember that means up to two and a half months of work that could have been used instead to bring disadvantaged people to your program as well as sell products and services to advantaged people at retail.

I know that working for ten dollar or even two hundred dollar sales doesn't bring the rush of receiving a five digit check in the mail, but you and your team have to realize that daily sales of hundreds and later, thousands of dollars will surpass the income you were able to raise through grants. This doesn't mean you should ever stop writing grants or asking for donations. This is one of the benefits of choosing a nonprofit structure. It simply means that you and your team must know when it's time to pull significant time and energy out of fundraising and place it instead into income generation. By doing so, your organization will become an important role model for the disadvantaged people you serve. They will see you working hard to create a great business that earns its income rather than pleading for charity assistance. This will inspire them to envision what sort of business they could create for themselves.

You will also face people, often on your board and staff, who argue against making profits, likely from that charity stereotype residue. They'll want to give the bikes and parts away rather than going through the arduous process of qualifying individuals for micro loans and/or subsidies. Some will even fight against charging full price to advantaged customers. I know this all too well from my days as a bike shop owner and operator. Some staff can't imagine charging full retail. But you cannot allow that bad behavior. Set your prices and ensure each of your staff sticks to them. You'll read more about pricing in Chapter 9.

If and when some staff and board members continue to argue for giving away your program's products and services, ask them, after more than four hundred years and the founding of millions of charity, volunteer-run nonprofits all over the world, why this struggling world of ours hasn't been cured. Until nonprofits can make this shift into social enterprises that engage and hire the very people they want to serve, such top down, detached charity concepts will flounder. The only way to make the shift is to recognize why corporations have succeeded so spectacularly in their flawed money grubbing vision and taken over this world of ours—profits. You and your fellow leaders will have to steer clear of the inevitable calls for charity practices and set out on an unfamiliar course for your Social Bike Business program that taps the profit making system of the corporations for social good. And that won't be easy.

Still, we have found the nonprofit structure to be the best so far for launching a Social Bike Business program. The first step is to found your organization with a mission statement that will encompass and justify sales of bicycles, bike parts and job training services for disadvantaged people. The legal wording in the U.S. is that any income generated from sales or services must be "substantially related" to the organization's purpose, that is, its mission statement. As I mentioned in the last chapter, such income must relate to the organization's mission, otherwise the organization must pay tax on that income. Be sure to read the section on Mission Statement in Chapter 2 if you missed it.

Some organizations that decide to take on the Social Bike Business program have already been incorporated as nonprofits. If this is your case, it can work well if your organization's mission will allow for income generated from the sales of bicycles and job training services. If it doesn't, you can file for a mission change, but that could be quite difficult. Or you could simply decide to pay the income taxes on that income.

I've worked with existing nonprofits that were founded as bicycle co-ops or collectives, but have become tired of the relentless struggle to stay open without any significant income. Leaders tend to get burned out in these organization structures and when they contact us, they are more than ready to learn how to shift into making profits and paying staff market wages. One nice thing about morphing from a volunteer-run bicycle co-op or collective into the Social Bike Business model is that the mission of the organization is quite likely to align with profit generation.

I've also received a few calls from leaders of bicycle advocacy organizations. None yet have taken on the program, but I can certainly imagine that this could work. The main danger is that the Social Bike Business program is extremely intensive and should never pull energy or resources away from advocacy efforts. So, only a very well-established bicycle advocacy organization that already has a strong paid staff and can support separate departments should even consider adding this program to their organization.

I need to offer a quick note here on a variation that could work for launching a Social Bike Business program. In some communities I've worked with, no single organization is prepared to take on the program, but a collaboration of several existing organizations sounds interesting to the leadership team. This can happen when the leadership team is comprised of leaders from several like-minded organizations. At this time in 2012, the few collaborative efforts I've assisted have ended with one of the organizations stepping up to lead the program. But this doesn't mean that a collaboration isn't possible. If a collaboration looks interesting to you and your fellow leaders, keep in mind that the program itself will have to have its own standalone name and retain a separate leadership team with representatives of each of the collaborating organizations.

Fiscal Sponsorship

In the next section I will describe the basic steps for incorporating a nonprofit. Before getting there, I want to offer a warning about a temptation that often derails nonprofits—fiscal sponsorship. In the U.S. and some other countries, the leaders of a new organization can choose to avoid incorporating by asking an incorporated nonprofit to become their "fiscal sponsor." This can look very enticing to new leaders who are already overwhelmed by all the tasks required to found an organization.

But don't be deceived! Fiscal sponsorship becomes a cozy arrangement that is very difficult to escape. The most harmful problem with fiscal sponsorship is that the "mother" organization must be mentioned in all communications. Also, all checks and credit card payments that go to your organization must be made payable to the mother organization, *not* yours. This means that all of your donors, grantors and customers will relate their experience with your program to the fiscal sponsor. If you and your fellow leaders eventually manage to break free of this fiscal sponsorship (and that's a big if), none of these important people will have any connection to your organization. In other words, once you break free and incorporate your organization independently, it will be as if you are starting from day number one.

The other danger of fiscal sponsorship is that the fiscal sponsor, or mother organization, does all the administrative work, including taking the credit for your organization, and simply charges a fee such as ten percent of all income that comes to your organization. This is of course fair because otherwise an established nonprofit could not justify taking on the burden of being a fiscal sponsor. Also, because of the high level of responsibility they have for your organization, you and your team will have to hand over some leadership of your organization to them.

Once you and your team have settled into this arrangement, most of you will be tempted to remain there in order to avoid the responsibility of learning how to do tax returns and sending reports to your funders. I know of some nonprofits that have operated under fiscal sponsorship for more than a decade and I can easily bet they will never break free. They will also remain small—the ones I know of are either run by volunteers or have just one, underpaid staff member.

TIP: Avoid fiscal sponsorship!

The most important danger of fiscal sponsorship in regards to Social Bike Business is that it will not allow the full implementation of the program. No fiscal sponsor would take on the responsibility and administration of such a complex program. Then consider that everything that includes the name of your organization must also show the name of the fiscal sponsor in order to give full disclosure. Imagine the sign you'll hang on the front of your bicycle community center... with *two* names. Imagine your brochures, business cards and custom price tags, all with *two* names of the organizations that run the program. Would you shop at a place with such a suspicious dual personality?

My recommendation regarding fiscal sponsorship is: Don't do it! And if you've unfortunately slipped into this cozy yet dangerous situation: Get out as soon as you can!

Incorporating as a Nonprofit

If you're just starting out and you and the others on your leadership team like the idea of a nonprofit structure, you'll want to begin the incorporation process right away. Until your organization is incorporated and receives its tax deductible status with your government, you cannot apply for grants. Also, most donors will avoid donating any significant amount of money, not only because they will not receive a tax deduction, but because your organization will not appear to be legitimate. The incorporation process requires several steps and often a lengthy waiting time until you receive your final notification, so the earlier you start, the better. But don't rush it.

First, make sure you and your team are working well together and describing the very same sort of organization. Make sure every leader is happy with the mission statement and the name you have chosen together for the organization. If any of the leaders are not supportive of these or feel like they have been left out of the process, you are not ready to move forward with incorporation. Instead, spend more time with your leadership team to work out discrepancies.

Once everyone is cheerfully taking part in the leadership team and happy with the mission and name of the organization it's nearly time to begin the incorporation process.

The next thing you should do is to seek out a professional who has helped other nonprofits incorporate in your country. While you and your team could likely navigate the process successfully, unless any of you have gone through it before, you will spend far more time than you would if you had the help of a professional. Most professionals like this will either be an attorney or an accountant, possibly a certified public accountant (CPA). But sometimes you will find a professional administrator working for a nonprofit who will also have the level of knowledge you'll need to make the process as easy as possible.

You will need to ask this professional if they can donate their services to assist your organization in this process. Such a professional service donation is often referred to as "pro bono." This will be your first major donor request because such an expert usually charges quite a bit of money for these services. However, most well established accountants and attorneys with nonprofit experience expect to serve several pro bono clients. This is a point of pride for them and something they like to report to their professional associations. But you'll still have to make a very good case as to why *your* organization should be one of the lucky ones they choose to serve pro bono. In Chapter 5 you will read more about making requests to donors. Read that section before making this significant request of a person who will likely remain extremely valuable for your organization well into the future.

At this point, I also recommend that you secure a business mailing address. You do not want your personal street address to be listed as the corporate headquarters for your organization. Not only will this seem suspicious to potential donors or partners, you also want to do everything you can to separate your organization from your personal life. If your organization doesn't have a street address yet, opening a post office box will work just fine. In fact, even after you open your bicycle community center or a separate office for administration you may choose to keep your post office box address. You might find that keeping your mail secure at the post office works better than having it delivered to a lively location where it can easily be misplaced.

Bylaws

One more item you will need before starting the incorporation process is your organization's bylaws. This document ensures that all leaders are working together toward the same purpose. Some organizations use their Articles of Incorporation as their bylaws, but I don't recommend this, at least in the U.S. This is because the U.S. requirements for Articles of Incorporation are convoluted, focused on financial conflicts of interest and operation details that qualify it for national nonprofit status. In contrast, your bylaws are your internal policies that you and future leaders will regularly refer to for leadership procedures. In order for your bylaws to serve this purpose well, they must be as short and concise as possible.

In fact, you can simply refer to your Articles of Incorporation in your bylaws and avoid repeating that language. The one repeated clause that both documents must include is your mission statement. Other than that, this will allow your bylaws to focus on how leaders are chosen, what responsibilities different leadership roles hold (make sure to include your executive director), removal of leaders not doing their job, the resignation process, and how amendments are made to the bylaws. If you choose to include term limits for board members, create a means for these committed and knowledgeable leaders to continue working with your organization.

I recommend a required full consensus of all leaders for approval of the removal of any leader and any amendment to the bylaws. However, if you and the others prefer majority vote, make sure that leader removal and bylaws amendments require a super majority of at least two thirds of all voting leaders if not three quarters. This will prevent wanton removals and amendments offered on a whim that could throw the organization into a tailspin.

Work as a team to ensure that your bylaws will cause the sort of leadership behaviors necessary for your organization to thrive. Beware of nonprofit bylaws templates that are circulating all over the internet and through well meaning, but lazy nonprofit coaches. Many of these bylaws templates include clauses that will eventually pit leaders against leaders. And most are so overburdened with legal language that not even an attorney can figure out what the original intention was. Your bylaws must use common language that all future leaders will clearly understand and be as short as possible. Leave out more specific policies that require frequent updates such as holding meetings, office operations and those better suited for your employee manual. For example, One Street's bylaws are just two concise pages. You can find them on our website under Our Leaders.

Tax Deductible Status

In the U.S., achieving recognition as a tax deductible nonprofit is a two step process—first at the state level, then at the national level. Most other countries will only have the national level step. For U.S. nonprofits, the state-level process is incredibly easy. Simply find the necessary paperwork for nonprofit incorporation through your state's corporation commission, fill them out and submit them with the required fees, usually less than one hundred dollars. But don't be fooled by the ease of this process. The required documents include your Articles of Incorporation that *must* have particular sections included in order for your nonprofit to qualify for the national level 501(c)(3) status you'll want. Work with your pro bono expert on your Articles of Incorporation as well as the other forms to ensure you have included all the required information for your nonprofit to qualify.

The 501(c)(3) status is just one form of nonprofit available at the national level in the U.S. Others such as 501(c)(4) for organizations that do a lot of lobbying and 501(c)(6) for business associations are also referred to as nonprofits, but they do not allow for tax deductions of donations. *Only* the 501(c)(3) nonprofit status will qualify you to apply for foundation grants and allow your donors to deduct their donations from their taxes.

This higher level status of the 501(c)(3) makes the paperwork quite a bit more complex than any of the other nonprofit types. It also comes with a much higher fee, close to one thousand dollars. Your application will also go through a much more thorough scrutiny at the IRS than applications for other types of nonprofits. Find the 501(c)(3) application forms at www.irs.gov.

Other countries follow a similar system at the national level causing the leaders of new nonprofits who want tax deductible status to go through a very extensive process and scrutiny. Work with your pro bono expert to find the necessary papers and carefully work through them before submitting.

Examples of Successful Nonprofit Social Businesses

Below I'll outline three highly successful social businesses that chose the nonprofit structure. All three have caught my eye as great models to learn from. They each represent a different budget level and serve communities in three different areas of the world.

HOMEBOY INDUSTRIES (*large budget*) – Los Angeles, California, USA

"Nothing stops a bullet like a job." Homeboy Industries' tagline captures the culture of this innovative social business. It was started as a simple jobs program in 1988 by an entrepreneurial pastor in one of the toughest neighborhoods in Los Angeles to offer alternatives to gang violence. The idea was to assist high-risk, recently released from prison, and formerly gang involved youth to become contributing members of their communities by responding to their complex needs. But the program soon grew beyond the parish.

Homeboy became an independent 501(c)(3) nonprofit social business in August of 2001 in order to expand into the multiple support services needed by the youth. Homeboy also offers jobs in a safe environment to the most challenging, difficult to place young people who complete their job-readiness programs. This helps them learn both concrete and soft job skills, while building their resume and work experience. Gang affiliations are left outside as these young people work together, side by side, learning the mutual respect that comes from shared tasks and challenges. From their renowned bakery, the central point of their social business structure, they've added complimentary businesses plus wraparound services including a charter high school, tattoo removal, educational classes, and solar panel installation training and certification.

Homeboy Industries is the largest gang intervention and re-entry program in the U.S. and is a model for similar programs around the world. Their budget now tops 14 million dollars each year and includes sales from their social enterprises, contributions from foundations and donors, and government grants. While they bring in nearly four million dollars in sales, seventy percent of their income still comes from contributions. Obviously this organization resonates with donors!

This is something to consider as you build the image of your organization. Does it look like a boring, institutional social program or does it grab people's heart strings as Homeboy Industries does? The difference can appear quite subtle to founding leaders. What if Homeboy Industries had chosen a name like Youth Jobs or the Alliance for Caring? What if they had chosen to locate in a rich neighborhood instead of the toughest part of their city where gangs thrive? What if all they offered these young people were one-way lecturing services that only delivered what well-to-do people thought they should hear? What if they hadn't made these former gang members the most important decision makers for their organization? I'm willing to bet they would not be bringing in over ten million dollars in contributions. More importantly, the thousands of youth they serve each year would likely not come near the place, making their nearly four million dollars in sales impossible. These differences may seem subtle, but they demonstrate why some organizations exceed their wildest dreams and others never come close to what their founders had envisioned.

Read more about Homeboy Industries on their website: www.homeboyindustries.org.

RICKSHAW BANK (*medium budget*) – Guwahati, Assam, India

Rickshaw Bank is a program of the Centre for Rural Development (CRD), a nonprofit organization. CRD was founded in 1994 to address livelihood opportunities through their broad agricultural intervention program in rural India. But in 2003, Dr. Pradip Kumar Sarmah, a veterinarian, CRD's Founder and Executive Director, took a fateful bicycle rickshaw ride in Guwahati. During the ride he asked the driver how much he made each day. The driver told him, but then explained that he must give most of the money he earns to the owner of the rickshaw. Dr. Sarmah spoke with others and learned these drivers often take the job because they are desperately poor. The rickshaw owners make them pay outrageous fees. Even worse, some of the owners give the drivers illegal drugs to help ease their physical pain and when they get addicted, they make them pay for these drugs, too.

It wasn't long before Dr. Sarmah was thoroughly horrified by the predicament of these bicycle rickshaw drivers. He learned that the situation was the same in cities all over India, affecting the nearly ten million rickshaws drivers in the country. He also traveled to Bangladesh to meet with Muhammad Yunus at Grameen Bank to learn about micro lending to help people buy into their own business.

In 2004, after careful planning, Dr. Sarmah and his team at CRD launched Rickshaw Bank to provide better bicycle rickshaws to drivers through a micro lending system that allowed them to fully purchase their own, quality rickshaw in just 18 months. Once they own their rickshaw they own their business. The program took off like wildfire, requiring rapid expansion in order to keep up with demand and has been growing ever since, including expansion into seven cities around India.

Not only are the loan payments lower than the rental fees the drivers had been paying the abusive owners, Rickshaw Bank also offers many benefits that bring them the dignity of being professional drivers. Some of these include insurance, licensing and uniforms. Rickshaw Bank also provides services to the drivers and their families including health care, family planning, training in life skills such as nutrition and saving money, and even emergency loans when crises hit. The program also helps the wives of the drivers start their own, complementary businesses such as selling food to the drivers at popular resting places.

As of 2012, Rickshaw Bank has served more than six thousand bicycle rickshaw drivers and their families. They have worked extensively with the Indian Institute of Technology to create a superior bicycle rickshaw that is thirty percent lighter than the old style. This new design is much more efficient and aerodynamic, saving the driver precious energy. It has a cover that protects the driver and passengers from sun and rain. It is much more comfortable for the passengers and provides them more luggage space.

Each bicycle rickshaw along with insurance, licensing and uniform costs a driver just under three hundred U.S. dollars, which they are supposed to pay off in 18 months. Each driver joins a group of five drivers, all of whom must ensure the others make their payments. Each group belongs to a garage with staff who help them work through difficulties. Each garage serves between 25 and 50 drivers. With this kind and supportive network, the repayment rate within 18 months is 92 percent.

Some drivers must take some more time to complete their payments and when the time is extended to two years, repayment is one hundred percent.

Rickshaw Bank is one of the best models I've found for creating diverse income streams. They receive income from ads on the back of their rickshaws, local governments contribute to the cost of each rickshaw, they charge their members an annual fee, they receive interest from their micro loans, and now they are experimenting with manufacturing carts for other small businesses such as fruit sellers and cargo transporters. They also attract grant funding and donations from around the world, which they put toward expanding their program.

Imagine all the different ways your program could tap diverse income sources once you begin your micro lending program for affordable, quality transportation bicycles for the disadvantaged people you want to serve.

Read more about Rickshaw Bank on CRD's web site for the program: www.crdev.org/rb.asp.

RIDE 4 A WOMAN (*small budget*) – Buhoma, Uganda

Most of the thousands of women in the region surrounding the Bwindi Impenetrable Forest spend their days and well into each night managing their households. They carry water, dig their family's garden, care for their children and animals, clean the house, and ensure everything is running smoothly. This leaves no time to learn a trade to earn money and very little time to learn from each other. On top of this, Ugandan culture discourages women from riding a bicycle or repairing anything. Their only form of self propulsion is to walk, which is six times slower than bicycling. Even though most Ugandan women and many men disagree with this taboo, the result is that few women have even tried to ride a bicycle or use mechanics' tools.

The leaders of Ride 4 a Woman (R4W) founded their organization in 2009 to tackle this problem. They chose the nonprofit Community Based Organisation (CBO) structure, Uganda's equivalent to the U.S.'s 501(c)(3). The mission they all rallied around was to empower the local women with bicycles, helping these women obtain their own transportation bicycle and teaching them mechanical skills by repairing bicycles. Along with this career training in mechanics, R4W envisioned many other career trainings in craft making, tailoring, and entertainment. They also realized that in order to help these local women break free of poverty they would need education in English and computers. While all of this might sound like ordinary nonprofit charity work, their vision was bona fide social business.

The Bwindi Impenetrable Forest National Park is home to the few remaining mountain gorillas left in this world. Tourists flock to Buhoma each year to pay five hundred dollars for the chance to see these gentle giants during half-day trekking outings with local guides. Though Buhoma is a tiny village just north of the park on a rough dirt road surrounded by rain forest, high-priced lodges have sprung up over the past ten years to accommodate these affluent visitors.

The founders of R4W recognized an income niche not yet tapped from these tourists. Many of the gorilla treks return by lunchtime leaving the tourists bored without other activities to engage in. The main trail through the forest is a former road with a reasonable grade, but still offers the full Bwindi forest experience. However, trained guides must accompany visitors. Mountain bike rentals and guided bike tours were a clear business opportunity. And because R4W's program work had to include bicycles and a comprehensive bicycle repair workshop, mountain bike rentals fit perfectly. This rental and guide service could then hire local women as mechanics and guides.

They launched their mountain bike rentals with just six used mountain bikes and as of 2012 have grown their fleet to 12. Now they are eyeballing a village south of the park where they can open a satellite bicycle rental business to tap the growing tourist trade down there. With the money raised through bike rentals, construction at their women's community centre is underway, but they haven't waited for its completion. They have offered classes to their over three hundred women members in bicycle riding, repair and tour guiding at a local elementary school when school isn't in session. These classes are so popular and the women so enthusiastic about their new skills that they can hardly wait to receive their own transportation bicycle. R4W has also hired some of these women to work as bicycle tour guides for their rental program. Others are selling crafts they've learned to make with R4W. And still others have been participating in R4W's Dance & Drama performances for tourists that generate money for the program and for the women performers.

R4W's next big step is to set up their micro lending program to ensure the sustainability of providing bicycles to their women members. They are studying successful micro lending programs similar to Rickshaw Bank's.

As they enter their fifth year, their budget remains quite small. Staff members are still only paid on a per job basis, which offers no job security and causes many of these skilled women to take jobs elsewhere. R4W's leaders are learning important promotion skills, refining their message and learning to ask for donations from tourists. In 2012, they are beginning their first coordinated grant writing effort with the hope of securing enough capital to complete both buildings of their women's community centre and outfit it with all the program tools and materials they need. When this is achieved, they can send the word out to the many other villages in the area and draw thousands more impoverished women to their career building programs.

R4W is one of the most courageous organizations I have worked with. They forge ahead with programs before all the optimum infrastructure and funding is in place. While such methods run the risk of failure or leader burnout, R4W's leaders remain committed to their eventual success and so roll through the inevitable difficulties. Because of their determination to provide their program services, they have logged significant successes that they can use to entice donors and foundations to give. How will you and your fellow leaders find a balance between forging ahead before everything is in place and waiting for support to come through?

Read more about Ride 4 a Woman on their website: www. ride4awoman.org.

All three of these examples offer inspiration for launching a Social Bike Business program. Their founders started by identifying the most disadvantaged people in their community and then fashioning their program to serve the particular needs of these people. As you and your fellow leaders discuss ideas for your organization and Social Bike Business program, remember these models and the high level of service to disadvantaged people they have achieved.

In the next chapter, you'll read more about planning and raising the capital you'll need to make your vision reality.

CHAPTER 4

Creating Your Plan

lanning is the most important responsibility for you and your fellow leaders because no one else will do it. Your plan is the only way to discover the steps your organization must take to reach effectiveness using the least amount of energy. Without a plan, you will waste enormous amounts of time and money dabbling in random activities and will likely lose many potential leaders and helpers along the way. No one stays around long without an effective plan.

But the planning process can also be the most detrimental activity you and your team engage in. Depending on your personalities, your team might rush planning to get to the fun action or all of you might be lulled into the all too common backwater of planning to plan in order to plan for more planning. I nearly fell out of my seat once at a bicycle conference when the speaker, Gil Penalosa demonstrated our tendency for over planning with a slide that said, "Ready, aim, aim, aim, aim...." You get the picture. Unless we fire, we won't help any disadvantaged people with bicycles. So, be sure to read this chapter carefully (but not too carefully...) and then move right onto the next on launching your program.

There are two types of planning you and your fellow leaders must engage in as long as you hold your leadership positions: long-term planning and annual planning.

Before I dig into each I need to mention that most of these concepts apply specifically to nonprofit organizations including having a board of directors, tapping fundraising, engaging volunteers, and such. But if you prefer to found your organization as a for-profit company, many of these concepts will still apply. Even as the sole leader, you will have to have a vivid idea of your long-term plan and spend significant time each year creating a detailed plan for the coming year.

Long-Term Planning

Long-term planning is like creating an imaginary map of your organization's world to hang on the wall at all of your board meetings. Each leader must see the exact same map to enable all of you to work as a cohesive governance team toward the same goals. The documents that result from it also must be clearly understood for easy reference. All of this can be accomplished during a few special meetings that set aside at least half a day each allowing all leaders to settle into the discussion and ensure all pertinent ideas are captured. Just as with all your board meetings, these planning meetings require a clear agenda that is sent in draft form to all leaders at least five days before the meeting (see Chapter 2 for more details on conducting productive meetings). Once you all have worked through the necessary discussions, capture your long-term plans in easy-to-use documents. Below I'll describe some of the most important ones for creating a strong organization that plans to take on a Social Bike Business program.

Mission/Vision/Values/Goals document:

This two to three page document will act as a backdrop for all your other planning activities and will help ensure all your plans align. It will also be your source for consistent messaging that will aid in the branding of your organization. You read in Chapter 2 about developing your mission statement, which is in fact your first step toward long-term planning because your mission sketches the boundaries of your organization's imaginary map. Simply having your mission statement (and name of your organization) will get you through the founding stage, including incorporation. These other sections—vision, values and goals—capture other viewpoints of your organization and ensure that each of you are working in the same direction. This document will also ensure that each of you can clearly explain your long-term expectations to potential funders, partners and helpers. The planning meetings that you and your team use to complete this document must be as laidback and interactive as the ones you used to create your mission statement. Set aside blocks of time of at least half a day and ensure that all leaders engage in the discussion.

TIP: Keep your mission statement to one, clear sentence.

Mission: One sentence that clearly states your organization's unique purpose, distinguishes it from others, and shows who it serves and where it serves. See more details in Chapter 2.

Vision: A one paragraph description of the community your organization serves *after* your organization has completed its work. Write it in present tense and an upbeat tone that captures the imaginations of all the founding leaders. Start from your mission statement. Be specific. Show all aspects of the results of your success. Your vision statement will act as a beacon even through the toughest times.

Values: A list of three to five guiding principles you all agree are important to the success of your organization. Your values will spring from the uniqueness of the community you serve, your particular backgrounds, and how you all view success. To ensure this document will set the stage for a strong Social Bike Business program, I recommend including at least one that emphasizes your priority service to the most disadvantaged people in your community.

Goals: This is the only section of the four that you must update every three years or so because you want to actually achieve your goals and move on to bigger ones. The first three sections are worth reviewing at that time, but are meant to offer long lasting guidance without the need for revisions. This section is for three to five general goals that align with the mission and could be achieved within three years. They should not include fine details. The detailed activities needed to achieve these goals will be developed during your annual planning, which I'll describe later in this chapter. Here's an example of a general goal: Ensure that a majority of the disadvantaged people in our community know about and feel welcome to engage with our organization. Such a general goal would necessitate several activities in your first year's annual plan such as promotions that reach into distressed neighborhoods, and landscaping, yard furniture or graphics in the front of your center that make it particularly welcoming to your community's disadvantaged residents.

Once all of you have completed your initial draft of your Mission/Vision/Values/Goals document, get input from others who have a keen interest in your organization. These can be potential clients, your experts, your helpers, and even friends and family members who can offer ways to clarify the language and ensure you've covered all the important concepts. Remember, this document, at least the first three sections, is meant to be used by many generations of leaders of your organization. Just because you and your fellow leaders understand it doesn't mean future leaders will. After you've received input from others, get that thesaurus out to replace any vague words with the words that do the most work capturing what all of you want to say. Once all of you are happy with it, formally approve it and add a note "Approved by Board of Directors on (*exact date including year*)."

A warning about tactics: Throughout this process, you and the others will voice ideas for particular activities. These activities, also called tactics, do not belong in this Mission/Vision/Values/Goals document. An example of a good long-term goal would be "Open our bicycle community center." Examples of tactics that would likely be voiced during the discussion of that goal include hiring a particular sign painter, scheduling a meeting with a landowner, building a bike parts cabinet, and getting a business license. But only "Open our bicycle community center" would be appropriate for the long-term document. All others must be discussed during the annual planning process. I guarantee that during these long-term planning meetings, several if not many great ideas for tactics will come out. Make sure to document them. Don't worry about defining or organizing them. Just list them separately on a "tactics" sheet for later reference when you're all ready to begin your annual planning process. But make sure all of you understand the difference between a long-term goal and a tactic because if your long-term goals are just a check list of activities that have no goal behind them, that Goals section will not be doing its job for you.

At this point I need to offer my next warning, this one about "strategic planning." The concept of strategic planning in itself is a good thing. In fact, the work you and your team do to create your Mission/Vision/Values/Goals document *is* strategic planning. Unfortunately, this term has been hijacked over the last ten years or so and is now often exploited by self-interested individuals, consultants and abusive funders. In its malignant form, strategic planning becomes an all consuming process. I have heard leaders of nonprofits describe grueling, overpriced, multi-year processes that distracted their organization from its work and only resulted in an extravagantly formatted book-length plan that says nothing. Others tell of tragedies that tore their leadership team apart.

Nonprofit consultants have raked in unimaginable profits by talking leaders into multi-year strategic planning contracts. Unethical funders have sidelined nonprofits by demanding they engage in extensive strategic planning before they will consider them for funding. And self-interested individuals who want to take control of a nonprofit have learned to demand strategic planning because they can easily hide their intentions behind this do-gooder demand as it derails the organization.

So, when you hear anyone asking for your organization to engage in "strategic planning," listen deeper for their intentions. Chances are they are using the term to describe healthy long-term planning such as what is involved in the creation of your Mission/Vision/Values/Goals document (above) or your business plan (below). In fact, if someone requests your strategic plan, these documents are sure to satisfy them. But if someone is asking you and your team to engage in an arduous process that would require hiring a consultant (perhaps themselves) and many months if not a few years to complete, step carefully away from that person and return the discussion to long-term planning in the best interest of your organization.

Business plan:

The next long-term planning document I recommend is your business plan. It must align with and include your organization's mission, vision, values and goals. It will detail the demographics of your community, show the income potential of tapping each segment, and reveal *expected* costs for ensuring a good portion of your community's residents buy products and services from your organization. I emphasize the word expected because no business plan can replace the careful oversight needed from a caring staff and board of directors once your program is launched. Unlike your mission, vision and values statements, a business plan must be updated every few years, especially in the beginning, to give you and your team a chance to compare your projections with actual accomplishments. From these comparisons, you will see where more energy and resources are needed and you'll find those surprising program elements that succeed far beyond expectations.

While your business plan will serve as an important internal planning tool, think of it mainly as a marketing tool. It can be a leave-behind for meetings with potential partners and funders. For instance, imagine approaching an owner of a property that would be perfect for your bicycle community center. You want to ask this owner if he or she would consider either donating their property for a tax write off or leasing it to your organization at a very low rate. This is a big request! Having a professionally prepared business plan that outlines how your Social Bike Business program will succeed can mean the difference between a breakthrough and a disappointment for your program.

There are many resources available on the internet and at your local library that will show you how to create a strong business plan. I've seen single-page business plans and ones that would break a sturdy table. Err on the shorter end of this spectrum. Just as with your bylaws and all your other planning documents, the most important thing is that your business plan is concise and easily understood. Even so, take note of these sections that are commonly expected in every business plan:

- Executive summary
- Business description (include mission, vision, values and goals in narrative)
- Business location with pertinent details
- Market definition including competition
- Products, including inventory sources, and services
- Organization and management including pertinent bios of leaders
- Marketing and sales strategy
- Financial management (includes your first year's annual budget and planning)

One of the easiest tools I've found for roughing out a business plan can be found on the U.S. Small Business Administration's website. Use their simple Business Plan Template to capture the absolute necessities http://web.sba.gov/busplantemplate/BizPlanStart.cfm. Once you have filled in each section, you and your team can refine your plan and take it to a professional printer for final design and printing. Spend the extra money to make it look very professional. You won't have to print very many, so it won't pinch your wallet too much.

Center Design:

Another long-term plan that will offer guidance for your team as well as inspiration for funders is the design of your bicycle community center. Whether or not you choose to launch your program with the opening of your bicycle community center, you'll want to work toward opening your center eventually. Also, the design of your center will be a fabulous fundraising tool. Passion for pummeling poverty, numbers of people to be served with bikes, and all the health and environmental benefits of bicycling will never stop a potential funder in their tracks like a design drawing of your center. Look for a volunteer expert who has access to architectural design software. Even a simple line drawing that shows room dimensions will be a great visual. If you can find a graphic designer to doll it up, all the better. You'll read more specifics about managing your center in Chapter 9 and the specifics on bicycle manufacture in Chapter 11. For now, include these absolute basics in your center design:

- Location in a distressed neighborhood that is easily accessed on foot and bike by most of the disadvantaged people in the community;
- Easy access from the street for pedestrians, bicyclists and drivers;
- Secure bike parking;
- A welcoming, professional storefront and outside seating;
- A glass front door or big glass windows that let newcomers see inside and enter and exit easily (fear of entrapment applies to all retail customers, but far more to impoverished people who are victimized more than other people);
- A welcome area where folks can sign up for a bike and/or career training that includes a bike safety check area and is staffed by a caring person trained through the program who lives in the neighborhood;
- At least two classrooms;
- Large repair area that allows separation of repair service and repair training;
- Separate bicycle manufacturing area even if this won't happen for several years; include welding, metal fabrication and painting areas; separate access for metal and supply deliveries; and ample storage area for steel, supplies and bicycles in manufacturing process;
- Separate storage area for donated bikes to be refurbished as well as newly manufactured bikes ready for sale;
- Bike riding skills training area outside, if possible.

Annual Planning

Near the end of each year, you and your fellow board members need to conduct a special meeting, at least half a day long, where you will examine your expectations for the year compared to what actually happened. Using this reality check, you will work together to develop your work plan and budget for the coming year. Reference your long-term planning documents to ensure the details you outline for the year will follow the shortest and most effective path toward your mission and general goals.

One decision you and your other board members will have to make is whether to use a calendar year or a different fiscal year. Most organizations operate under a calendar year that starts January 1st and ends December 31st. But others choose to start July 1st and end June 30th or start October 1st and end September 30th. There are various reasons for choosing such odd fiscal years, usually to align with similar organizations. For instance, many local governments in the U.S. use the July to June year to align with the government budgeting process. Unless there is an important reason to do otherwise, I recommend you stick with the calendar year.

Annual Work Plan/Budget:

This document must be created new for each year and is meant to be referenced so frequently that printed copies will be worn out by the end of the year. It must be short enough, two to four pages is ideal, that all leaders and key staff of the organization can easily refer to it to ensure they are on track. Imagine copies of it jammed in back pockets or stapled to walls above monitors. It should come out at every board meeting for reference and it will become your basis for funding proposals. Prohibit jargon. Use common language and choose only words that bring clear meaning. Delete the rest.

You'll note that I do not separate work plan and budget. Separating these two is always a big mistake. They must be inseparably linked, each section and line dependent on the other. Even during the meeting when the board creates this document, make sure the discussions flow easily between work (activities you'll undertake) and the money necessary to make that work possible. During my on-call assistance work at One Street, I can't count the number of times I've discovered separate work plans and budgets as the cause of organization chaos. It's too easy to outline wonderful tasks for your organization without considering their costs or where the funding will come from. On the other side, it's too easy to blindly set numbers into an Income/Expense spreadsheet without having to dissect each planned activity for its costs and income potentials. Combining and aligning the two is certainly more work, but you will end up with a document that is based on reality and a quality tool for success.

The budget section can be at the start of your Work Plan/Budget document as a simple overview, though it must capture all expenses and income potentials revealed in the work plan section. In a few pages, you will read about a budget cash flow chart, which is a very handy way to pull apart your budget into a more detailed, living document that will allow you to compare your budget to what actually occurs each month. In Chapter 9 you'll read about more bookkeeping systems that will track sales, inventory, payroll and other complex line items. But for now, until you open your bicycle community center, these simple documents will do the trick. Even after you add the new bookkeeping systems, the process of annual planning will remain the same. The bookkeeping system will help you refine your annual work plan/budget, but won't replace it.

So what is a budget? Most importantly, it is only a projection. However, it is a concise projection that must come close to reality in order for it to be useful. It must have two sections—income and expense—and either be "balanced," which means the income and expense totals are the same number, or strive for an income surplus. Because the Social Bike Business program needs to ramp up over several years, I recommend planning for budget surplus. If a potential funder or partner asks for your organization's budget, chances are they are simply asking for a number. If you have a balanced budget, that will be the number that shows on both the income and expense total lines. If your budget shows a surplus, give them the expense number because that is what you plan to spend that year.

An organization's first few budgets are often a bit off. Sometimes leaders will shoot too high, expecting everyone who's excited about their new organization to contribute or that most of the grants they apply for will come in. Other leadership teams shoot too low and when unexpected funding comes in, they have to scramble to plan for its appropriate expenditure. Be sure to set a policy for adjusting your budget. This policy must make the process a bit arduous in order to prevent constant tweaking that will result in too many versions and confusion over which budget you're all following. I always recommend that at least one thorough budget review and adjustment process takes place halfway through the year. If you're on target, it will be an easy meeting. If not, make sure you set aside enough time to do a good job so that you and your team will have a trustworthy document to follow for the rest of the year.

On the next page is a simple example of a Work Plan/Budget for a young organization planning to launch their Social Bike Business program in the coming year. You will likely start with one that covers the costs of raising capital, setting up systems, and creating your plans before you're ready to open your center. But I wanted to show some active program line items. The budget is heavy on contributions. Keep in mind that as your program gains popularity, your sales and service income should outpace your contributions, at least your grant income. You and your team can choose a different format that better fits your needs. But keep your work plan and budget combined and take the time needed to examine every activity you plan in order to capture every cost and income potential.

(org name) Work Plan/Budget (year)

INCOME

Supporters	$20,000
Sponsors	$10,000
Grants	$50,000
Sales	$10,000
Microloan interest	$1,000
Service/Training fees	$4,000
TOTAL:	$95,000

EXPENSE

Payroll	$45,000
Payroll expense	$15,000
Health insurance	$6,000
Building renovation	$15,000
Repair area supplies	$2,000
Bike parts	$2,000
Utilities	$1,500
Website	$500
Printing	$1,000
Postage & Shipping	$500
Phone	$650
Supplies & Services	$750
Transportation	$500
Fees & Dues	$200
TOTAL:	$90,600 (this leaves over $4,000 for surplus for next year)

OPENING CENTER
Add text that includes center design, building construction/renovation, furnishings, sign, parking for cars and bikes, outside riding skills course, landscaping, and other activities needed to open.

CENTER WELCOME AREA
Include staffing, supplies, promotions and other operations needed to make your welcome area the best it can be.

BICYCLE DONATIONS & REFURBISHING
Include staffing, outreach for bikes, storage costs (ideally your center will have storage capacity), repair area supplies, new bike parts, etc.

MICRO LENDING & SUBSIDY SYSTEM
Include program set up, staffing (could be a percentage of welcome area staff), grant writing and fundraising for subsidizing bikes for most needy (or include in fundraising section below), partner institution costs and time needed, etc.

CAREER TRAINING
Include staff time for registering students, class room supplies, training staff and training supplies needed.

ADMINISTRATION
Include management staff, contracting with experts, website, and bookkeeping.

FUNDRAISING & PROMOTION
Include mailings, social and fundraising events, grant writing, writing press releases and other fundraising and promotions activities.

Adjust the budget line items to include all expenses identified in each work plan section.

Budget/Actual cash flow chart:

Your budget/actual cash flow chart will be an excellent tool for tracking your progress throughout the year and ensuring you spend only money that is available. While the above Work Plan/Budget example works well as a Word or similar document, your cash flow chart will work best in Excel or a similar spreadsheet. This format will clearly show your projected expenses through the whole year to help you avoid spending money that is needed in a later month. You'll add several more line items than your work plan/budget shows, breaking out each budget item into specifics. For instance, you'll break "payroll" into a row for each staff member. You might also want to section off different sub-programs such as career training and repair service so you can track their income and expenses more clearly.

Find an example of a cash flow spreadsheet complete with calculating formulas on One Street's website under Management in the left menu. Note that it was created with a typical bicycle advocacy organization in mind so many of the row titles won't apply to your organization. You can use this example to create your Budget/Actual cash flow chart by adding an unchanging column, separate from the calculating formulas, to the left of the "actual" column and inserting your budget figures. This added column will help you compare your projected budget to what is actually happening each month.

As I mentioned earlier, you'll read about more sophisticated bookkeeping software in Chapter 9 such as Quickbooks and Point-of-Sale (POS) systems. But if you do a good job of organizing this spreadsheet, you'll have an easier time setting up these systems later on. And as you begin to raise money to launch your program, this system will help you do a good job of tracking donations, grants and sales income. You might want to show this spreadsheet to your pro bono accountant to get their advice on rows to include.

Designing Your Program

Now that you know *how* to plan, you need to consider *what* to plan. Remember that your program is unique and should only include what makes sense for it. Also note that no Social Bike Business program will ever start with every possible program element in place. Some may never implement all the elements. Some launch without their center open by partnering with other organizations and vocational schools. Others are started by established organizations already located in a functional building that suits the program. Some launch in communities desperate for quality, affordable transportation bicycles. Others launch in communities desperate for career training. As I discussed in Chapter 2, do everything you can to involve your community's most disadvantaged people from the start. They will let you know their priority needs. Then choose the program elements that will take care of their urgencies and set up your program to add more.

For instance, if you want to launch your program before your center is open, look for partners who can help your program in the long run. Even if an excellent vocational school offers you the use of a classroom for a low fee, but they aren't interested in helping beyond that year, seek out a more committed partner before moving ahead. Another example might be a kindhearted property owner that offers the use of their building, but their building is in an affluent neighborhood. You don't want to snub your priority clients from the start by choosing an inappropriate location even if it is a great deal.

A similar temptation to guard against is called "chasing the money." The scenario is a funder who will only fund your program if you divert your efforts away from what you and your fellow leaders have planned. For instance, a rich donor might be obsessed with bike share programs and ask you and your team to develop and manage such a program with their donation. Bike share programs are free bikes for tourists and commuters; in other words, affluent people who have jobs and can afford vacations. This funder might be offering hundreds of thousands of dollars to your organization, but if you take the bait, you will have to shut down your Social Bike Business program in order to serve the tourists and commuters well.

If all of you are simply in this to do anything fun with bikes, such an offer might be worth taking. Bike share programs are a terrific way to encourage advantaged people to try bicycling. But if all of you are truly committed to defying poverty with bicycles, you will have to turn down this offer. Perhaps you could suggest to this donor that if he or she manages to get the bike share program started, your organization might be a good fit for servicing the bike share bikes as part of your job training program. It's always best to discuss options with people who offer funding. But if a donor is dead set on a specific use of their money and it doesn't fit your long-term plans, you must walk away. If you want to succeed with your Social Bike Business program plan, do not chase the money!

With all of your planning documents fleshed out and polished you're nearly ready to approach potential funders. As you and your fellow leaders likely discovered during the planning processes outlined earlier, you'll need a significant amount of money before you can comfortably invite disadvantaged people to take part in your program. You don't want to invite lots of folks to come to you and then have only a few bikes or maybe just one or two classes to offer. First impressions are extremely important to building a good reputation for your organization and program. This isn't only a concern for the first people who show up. They will tell all their friends and family if they had a bad experience and such a damaging report can spread throughout a community like wildfire. I've heard that people are twelve times more likely to tell others about a bad program experience as they are to tell about a good one. So decide on that minimum funding amount you'll need to do a good job with your first clients and make sure you raise it before promoting your program's launch.

We'll look into various ways you can raise the initial capital you'll need to launch your program in the next chapter. But first, a few final tasks to ensure you're ready for fundraising.

Three Tasks Before Raising Capital to Launch Your Program

1) <u>Open a bank account for your organization</u>. No significant funder will contribute to an organization that does not have a bank account. Choose a local bank or credit union you feel comfortable working with. The people who work there will become some of your best experts when you are ready to launch your micro lending program. You'll need to have your basic incorporation filing finished because they will ask for your organization's corporate number and other specifics.

2) <u>Launch your organization's website.</u> Funders considering contributing to your organization will first look for your website. Websites have become another storefront for organizations, so make sure it represents your organization well. Find a local expert in website development to help. Here are a few specifics I recommend:

- Choose a Content Management System (CMS) format instead of the old style HTML. A CMS website format such as Joomla or Drupal, will allow all of you to easily update your site without having to pay a web designer just for updates. Regular updates are extremely important to keep your site fresh and encourage visitors to return.
- Do not settle for a free blog site. While these are tempting because they are free, having such a site sends the message that you are not committed to investing in your organization, that it is only temporary. You can add a blog section to your website after the site is established, but don't make it the main site.
- Study sites that impress you and note the layout details you want for your own site. Have as few pages and menu items as possible and avoid drop down menus as they only confuse visitors.
- Keep text to the bare minimum. Choose your words carefully so visitors do not have to scroll to find the important information on each page.
- Break up text with images. At first, these might be photos of planning meetings and your early gatherings to form the organization. Later you can add photos of clients receiving their bike, learning repair and engaging in career training.

- Finalize your organization's logo before launching your website so you can include it as part of the template that shows on every page.
- Include a Who We Are or About Us page that lists the names of each of the leadership team members and a few sentences about each. Later you can add staff to this page. Anyone considering helping an organization needs to know who is leading it.
- Include a Donations page and a very visible "DONATE" button on every page that links to it. Briefly include on this page why donations are important and what the funding will go toward. Then show visitors *how* they can donate. At the minimum, include your organization's mailing address where they can send a check. If you are outside of the U.S., bank transfer might be a common way to donate so add all the bank transfer details and numbers they'll need. Eventually, you'll want to add to your site a sophisticated credit card payment system that goes directly to your bank account. These cost extra to set up and bank fees on top of that. Still, this is better than sending people away from your site to pay through another service such as PayPal. But until you can afford it, PayPal or similar will work fine. They also charge a fee.
- Include another link on every page for visitors to sign up for your e-newsletter. This can be as simple as connecting the link to a page that describes your e-newsletter with a request for them to email you to sign up. If you choose to use an outside emailing service for your e-newsletters you and your web designer can also set up a way for visitors to add themselves to the list with only your approval needed to finish the addition. If you use such a system, include a way to block spammers.
- Most web hosting services will offer free email addresses. This will allow each of you to create an email address with your organization's web address, which gives a professional impression.

3) Create a donor record system. As you will read in the next chapter, individual donors commonly like to give every year, but before they give again, they first expect to be asked. Without a system to track donations, you could be missing out on many years of repeat donations that can add up to lots of money for your organization's work. See Chapter 2 for details on setting up a simple spreadsheet that will keep you on track for inviting your donors to give year after year.

Now, with these systems in place and your team fired up to do some major fundraising, it's time to dig into a variety of fundraising activities. Read on to learn about some of the most successful methods of raising initial capital.

CHAPTER 5

Raising Capital to Launch Your Program

Preparing to raise the capital you need to launch your program can be daunting. You have a big number and seemingly no way to reach it. I hope I can ease that concern in this chapter and show you that this important early step will be one of the most rewarding as you connect with the people who want to help your program succeed.

Most of the fundraising concepts I'll offer in this chapter apply mainly to nonprofits. But even for-profit social businesses will find some ideas in them. Also, for-profit companies have the added potential of attracting venture capitalists who can invest in your company with the caveat that they then own part of the company. This means you will need to share any profits with them and you will have to follow strict procedures to qualify for such transactions. In the U.S., you'll need to register with the Securities and Exchange Commission: www.sec.gov. A venture capitalist might also consider a straight loan, which you can pay back with interest and no ownership strings. If you know venture capitalists, this could be an option. Otherwise, this will be a long shot. Plus, this is usually not an option for nonprofits as most venture capitalists expect a for-profit structure. Discuss this with your pro bono attorney before moving forward with such a deal.

Now for all those fun fundraising potentials for nonprofits. Before you begin, make sure all your long-term plans and your annual work plan/budget are ready for show time. These documents will contain all the answers to common questions funders might ask and will give you what you'll need to complete comprehensive funding proposals.

One important general rule in fundraising, whether for initial capital or ongoing program funding, is to have as many diverse sources of funding as possible. For a Social Bike Business program these can include sales and service income, donations from supporters, sponsorships, government contracts, and grants from several different foundations. At One Street we hear far too often about nonprofits flung into chaos or even shut down completely because a funding source didn't come through. Perhaps an expected grant is rejected or a long-term government contract is cut off. Had they had other funding sources they could have shifted funding expectations to them and weathered the blow.

Keep in mind that all fundraising is people giving to people. Whether you are asking your aunt for a donation or writing a ten page grant proposal for a massive foundation, the most important element of any funding request is your personal connection to the people who will decide whether or not to give. So, for all your grant proposals, all your sponsorship requests and all your government contract applications, make sure to first connect with the decision makers. If possible, sit down with them, buy them lunch, or just arrange to meet them for half an hour at their office. This personal connection will set your proposal out from all the others they receive and it will give it a better chance of success. So, as you read about the "Direct Ask" on the next page, remember that the concepts I describe in that section also apply to all the other fundraising sections that follow.

On the same note, remember that all the fundraising concepts in this chapter will apply not just to your early efforts to raise capital, but to your ongoing fundraising efforts. As you forge ahead with these efforts, the connections you make and the lessons you learn will benefit your Social Bike Business program on into the future.

One example of this will come from the necessity to set up several methods for donors to give, even at this early stage. Every one of these devices will continue to bring donations to your organization after your program is up and running. Make donating easy for people who want to help and give them a selection to ensure you've included their preferred method of donating. Remember that every potential donor will have the option of choosing not to give. In fact, most donations are impulse decisions. Think of all the times you've given to charities and you'll realize you decided to give moments before you gave. The longer it takes for a donor to figure out how to give to your organization, the more likely they are to change their mind.

The three most common donation methods are: an online credit card donation system (PayPal or similar will work fine at the beginning), a mail-in form for them to send along with their check (post this online for them to print and use it as a handout), and a way for them to hand deliver their donation. With all of the donation methods you create, make sure they include a form that captures the donor's full name, their mailing address, email address, donation amount and the date they donated. A phone number is also a good idea in case there's a problem with their donation. Then enter all of this information into your donor tracking system.

Follow up every online or mailed in contribution with a letter of appreciation that specifies the amount they gave and notes your organization's tax-deductible status (if you have received it) so they can use the letter when they file their taxes. The main body can be a form letter you refresh each year with highlights about your current programs showing how their donation will help. But make sure the first paragraph is personalized for them. You might also like to have a donation receipt system at your center for people who donate money, bikes and other supplies in person. If they receive such a receipt there's no need to send them a letter. Just be sure that every donor's contribution is recorded with all their contact info and the exact date, and that they receive a letter or receipt for their tax records.

The Direct Ask

The direct ask is the simplest type of fundraising. You find people who are passionate about your organization's work and simply ask them for a significant donation. However, while it is simplest logistically, it can actually be the most difficult. Few nonprofit leaders jump for joy when given the opportunity to make a direct ask of a potential donor. If your gut wrenches with the very thought of asking for a donation, don't worry. You're not alone. There must be something in our DNA that tells us we are not allowed to ask for help from anyone.

Here's how you address that gut twist: Keep in mind that by asking potential donors for a donation, you are offering them an opportunity to contribute significantly to their community. Most people have every second of their lives scheduled. Your suggestion to give is their opportunity to make a real impact by supporting the work of your organization. They make the donation to enable you and your team to help people with bicycles; work they simply could not do themselves. So first, change your mindset from asking for help to offering donors an opportunity to help their community. Then remember: They can't say "yes" unless you ask!

Here are the top reasons the direct ask is the most effective way to raise funds for your organization:

1. There's no need for expensive printing—the donor will rely on you for answers.
2. Donations and pledges can be given immediately.
3. Donor funds can be used where your organization needs them most.
4. Happy donors often give year after year.

There are many ways to find potential donors to help launch your program. Ask active people in your community if they know of people who would like to support the launching of your program. Scan lists of donors of like-minded organizations. Attend fundraising events and meet the people in your community who tend to donate to great causes. And always keep your eyes and ears open for people inclined to give money. Have the rest of your leadership team do the same. If your organization is well established, look back in your records for donors who gave fifty dollars or more. There's a good chance they might like to make a larger donation, especially to help with this exciting new program.

Before reaching out to a potential donor, make sure they are likely to be interested in your organization's Social Bike Business program work. Have they supported programs that fight poverty? Do they like bicycles? Perhaps they volunteer at a jobs fair each year. Such details can show you they are a potential donor and give you conversation starters when you sit down with them. Do a bit of research to find out what level of contribution they have given in the past. Sometimes organizations post the names of their donors categorized by their general level of support. Don't just look at the current year, but way back. This is especially important for your organization. If your organization has been around for awhile, you might find a major donor gave one thousand dollars ten years ago and never gave again.

One of the top reasons donors stop giving is because no one asked them to give again. This can happen when their contact info changes. Try to avoid this by noting address changes immediately. If you send out postal mailings to all your supporters, send some first class rather than with the nonprofit rate so you will receive address change notifications. Far worse is if your organization simply neglected to contact donors again. Remedy this right away. Send them updates and newsletters, let them know about upcoming activities. Then send them an appeal for another donation at least once a year. If they appear to be a potential major donor, ask them with a direct ask.

Once you have done your research on your potential donor, it's time to prepare for the initial call. Have all your planning documents in front of you to answer any questions they might have. Practice describing why you contribute your time and money to your organization so you can demonstrate your own commitment.

Keep in mind that this initial call is not the place for the funding ask. The only ask you will make here is for them to meet with you (and perhaps one other person from your organization) to discuss their financial support of your organization. Show your appreciation of their interest in your organization and any support they have given to yours or similar efforts in the community. Make sure they know the meeting is to discuss a donation (don't mention a specific amount at this point) and let them know half an hour should be plenty. This will allow them to prepare for the meeting. Ask them how, where and when they prefer to meet. If they would like to do lunch, expect to pay the entire bill whether they decide to give or not.

On the day of the meeting, bring all your notes and planning documents. Show up on time or even a bit early. Keep your presentation under five minutes. Remember, this meeting is about *their* interests, not yours.

You only have half an hour so keep the discussion focused. Ask questions so you can learn their hopes and dreams and how they would like to invest their money in the community. Briefly interject details about how your organization is helping disadvantaged people with bicycles. Align these details with this donor's needs, noting areas where funding is needed i.e., "Ah, you are interested in creating a place where people can come to learn about bicycling. We are actually hoping to raise enough money this year to open our bicycle community center." (This of course is in your work plan already.) Repeating part of what they say in your questions and comments, as in the above example, is an important way to show them you are listening.

Do not give them anything to read during the meeting. This will only distract them from the discussion.

Watch the clock! Make the ask before the half hour is up or, if it's lunch, well before the check arrives (and remember, you're paying whether they decide to give or not).

When it's time for you to make the ask, note a specific connection discovered during the meeting between their interests and the work of your organization. Make sure this pertains to work your organization is already committed to. Be clear that the money will be used for your organization's current, planned needs (remember: never chase the money). Include a specific amount, taking into account the research you did on their previous contributions and financial ability. Also remember that you could be meeting with a property owner, a for-profit bike shop owner, an expert or someone who could donate needed supplies. Your ask could be for services, supplies, a property donation or a very cheap lease, so don't get stuck on monetary donations. Study your work plan for that year to see if such "in-kind" donations would fit. Here's an example of a direct ask for money:

"Well, I think we've found some exciting connections here today. It looks like our organization is addressing many of your needs through our Social Bike Business program, especially with our work to establish our bicycle community center. Could you contribute five thousand dollars toward the renovation of the building that was recently donated to us?"

After the ask: *Do not say a word*! This is perhaps the most critical tip of all. You must let them think. Do not make the mistake of assuming their silence means they are upset. It simply means that you have asked them for a lot of money and they need to run some figures before they can answer. Let them be the next to speak.

If they agree, show your gratitude and commit to personally keeping them updated on the progress—note this in your calendar and make sure it gets done.

They might ask to give a smaller amount. This is great because you'll know you didn't ask for too little. Thank them and commit to keeping them updated.

They may write a check right there. If not, let them know that you or one of your organization's staff will send them a letter soon requesting their pledge and noting some of the details from the meeting for their records.

They might ask for more specifics in writing, even a full proposal, before they commit. This is fine, too, because it isn't a "no." Ask them what specific information they'd like to see in this letter or proposal and take detailed notes. Then, make sure you send this to them as soon as possible after the meeting, starting it with your gratitude to them for meeting with you.

TIP: A "no" can turn into a "yes" later, if you take good care of your potential donors.

They might say no. That's okay. Remember, you'll never get a "yes" unless you ask and that always comes with some "no"s. Be very gracious, thank them for their time and offer another way they can contribute—perhaps dropping by to check on your progress, acting as an on-call consultant or simply spreading the word to their friends. They'll be feeling far worse than you, so do your best to ease their mind about their decision. If they aren't a donor today, they can still become one in the future.

Send a handwritten thank you note by the next day no matter what their answer was, simply thanking them for the meeting. This is separate from any additional written details they may have requested.

After you receive their donation, immediately send a professional thank you letter which they can use for their records. If you have received your nonprofit tax deduction status with your national government, note this in the letter so they can use it when they file for a tax deduction. This letter will also help to build your relationship with this donor. Think of it and your future communications as an unbroken thread that allows them the opportunity to continue to support your organization.

Show appreciation for their donation in your materials and on your website, where appropriate. These general accolades and communications such as print and email newsletters, advocacy alerts, event notices, and such, add to the substance of your relationship with this donor. But remember, these gestures do not replace your direct, personal connections with them. Always make room in your schedule for direct contact with your major donors, even if it's just a personalized update on their favorite programs. Such updates show them you value them as a partner without asking them too often for a donation. One request per year of each major donor is plenty.

Also, look for special ways to involve your donors. This could include asking for their advice or personally inviting them to an event or ribbon cutting that includes their interest. Once you get the knack for the direct ask, you'll find you enjoy connecting with these folks because they share your passion and appreciate you showing them how their contribution is helping your organization's work.

And remember: Ask them again next year! If you don't, they'll be disappointed, maybe even insulted. Donors want to give. Make sure you give them that opportunity by asking.

Fundraising Events

Fundraising events require a tremendous amount of time and resources, so don't take one on unless you and your team are sure of success. They do bring one important benefit that none of the other fundraising methods have—gathering important people together to help your organization. Great events can solidify donors' commitments to help your organization. Your donors have fun, they learn more about your organization, they meet all the leaders, and they see their colleagues and friends also offering their support. This can be very powerful for long-term relationship building. But every event also comes with a serious risk—if it flops, the potential donors who do attend will leave with a bad impression of your organization and, as I mentioned earlier, they are even more likely to spread a bad report to their friends and colleagues. Take this risk seriously and be sure you and your team can pull off your event before moving forward.

Successful fundraising events always have talented people at their helm. Make sure that either you or someone on your team possesses that unique quality necessary to host an enchanting event. Don't move ahead until you've received such a commitment, especially from someone who has led fundraising events in the past. Besides the event leader, you will need a team of helpers tasked with various specialties depending on the type of event you are planning.

As you and your fellow leaders discuss your event plans, don't forget to differentiate between social events and fundraising events. This is a fundraising event, not just a social event. Each of you must fully understand this distinction and ensure that all of your promotional messages clearly show this distinction. For instance, if you want to hold a bike ride to raise funds, call it a fundraising ride, not just a fun ride or social ride. The same applies for a dinner. You need the people who attend to expect to donate. If your ride or dinner is filled with people who just want to have fun, the event will cost your organization money rather than raising funds. Social events are certainly something to consider adding to your program once it is well established, but never confuse them with fundraising.

No matter what sort of event you organize, charge a ticket price well over the amount needed to cover all costs, assuming you sell your minimum (you'll need to do a detailed event budget to know this amount). Clearly describe what their donation will go toward. If your event includes an auction, make sure you still charge an entry fee. Perhaps add a raffle and games they pay to play because typically only ten percent of attendees will bid on items. Lay a donation envelope on each plate so quiet attendees will have an easy way to donate. Offer many ways for them to contribute. Just as with the direct ask, you must be clear about the reason for the gathering and ask for enough money to make it truly beneficial to your organization's needs; and worth all the time and resources it requires. Clearly showing it is a fundraiser will ensure that people who can afford to contribute will fill your event.

Another rule to keep in mind is that any fundraising event requires a *minimum* of six months to plan and prepare, one full year is better. Gathering your helpers, securing the event location or permits for a ride, promoting the event to people who can afford to donate, and organizing supplies, speakers and food take an enormous amount of time. Just as with the organization planning procedures outlined in Chapter 4, take the time to list all the necessary people, supplies and steps you'll need to succeed. Then carefully place these in a conservative timeline that allows for setbacks. You'll see that six months will be pushing it.

These rules apply to any fundraising event. However, there is one creative exception: Stay at home "events." These are not actually events, rather a clever way to inspire people to give. I've never personally tried one of these, but I've heard of other organizations succeeding surprisingly well with them. The idea is to announce a lavish "event" including the date and time and all the activities, but the place is at the reader's home. You could call it a single family dinner or a private fundraising ride. All they really need to do is send in their donation, but you could offer a way for participants to upload their creative ideas, photos of their "event" or ride, and other fun activities onto your website and social media sites. Of course this will save you time and money on event costs, but you will still need to do the same amount of promotion and ensure it reaches people who can give.

Do ample research into the type of event you would like to organize before starting your effort. Seek out event planners in your community who can offer ideas. And don't forget to track down that all important, energetic event leader before you start.

Sponsorships

Sponsorship is just a fancy form of advertising for companies. As advertising has become a constant blur in all of our lives, companies are learning that their advertising budget is better spent placing their name and logo with nonprofits and their activities. They expect to pay, usually from their advertising budget, so charge an appropriate amount.

Research sponsorship levels of other nonprofits in your community and either round down or up depending on how your organization compares to the others. For instance, a large nonprofit might own a property on a busy road where they could post a sign thanking their sponsors, plus run TV and radio ads with their sponsors' names and logos. You likely won't have the funds to offer such fabulous advertising. But you will have a website, an e-newsletter and perhaps can make a banner thanking sponsors, which you can hang at events or at your center.

Potential sponsors need to know exactly where their logo will be seen and by whom. They only care that their particular potential customers see their logo and learn about their company's support of your organization. A bike shop owner is going to be a lot more excited about a banner with their logo being hung at the end of a bike ride than they would about it being hung on a wall at the local library. A natural food store owner will be more interested in college students seeing their logo than the annual gathering of ranchers.

Another important tip is to always give sponsorships a time limit. If you're requesting sponsorships for an event, perhaps your fundraising event, let them know that the promotions with their company name and logo will only go through the event. If you request general sponsorships, let them know exactly when and how you will display their company name and logo. Never go longer than a year because you want to ask them again each year.

Places where you can display sponsor names and logos include:

- Your organization's website (keep home page sponsors small and to a minimum because you don't want them to overshadow your logo),
- Banners and T-shirts,
- Events, including social events, but also fundraising events,
- Print material (place their logo on the back with a "Thanks to:" note),
- Inclusion in a press release and newsletter article.

Requesting sponsorships is just like the direct ask, except this is a business deal. Do the research and then request the meeting. You will be asking for a portion of their advertising (or marketing) budget. A potential sponsor will need to know specifics about your organization and the audience that will see their logo. Before arranging the meeting, honestly assess the value of sponsoring your organization. How many people recognize your organization and know what it does? Is your organization's reputation truly good in the eyes of this sponsor's target customer base? Do you have multiple channels for displaying their name and logo? If you and your team can confidently answer these questions in the positive, sponsorships are likely a good addition to your fundraising portfolio.

When you meet with a potential sponsor, in addition to all your planning materials, bring along details such as:

- Where their logo will be displayed and for how long,
- The demographics of the people who will see their logo and why they are likely to buy their products,
- Details about the work of your organization and how their sponsorship will help.

The best book I have found on the topic of sponsorships for nonprofits is *Made Possible By: Succeeding with Sponsorship* by Patricia Martin. The author covers all aspects of what nonprofits must do to compete for sponsorships including nonprofits with multi-million dollar budgets. Even though much of the book will not apply to smaller nonprofits, understanding the expectations of sponsors will help you make appropriate sponsorship requests.

Grants

Foundation grants are the most compelling way to raise capital because they seem to be less time consuming than other methods and can end in the receipt of a big check. Don't be fooled!

Grant writing is not much different than the direct ask because you must do that early research to understand the foundation's needs, how much they typically give and their preferred way to receive a request. But they lack the most important part of the direct ask—direct connection between you and the funder. In fact, over the years most foundations have erected massive barriers between themselves and grant seekers. I suppose this is simple survival. With more than 1.5 million nonprofits registered in just the U.S. alone and only 120,000 foundations in the U.S. to absorb their funding requests, the odds are stacked against them. This ratio is similar around the world as the number of nonprofits grows, so all foundations are barraged with funding proposals. On top of this, grant writing consultants spent the last decade telling rooms full of nonprofit leaders that the best way to get their proposal funded was to personally speak with someone at the foundation. To protect themselves from the onslaught of phone calls and requests for meetings, foundations have shut off all contact with grant seekers. Many no longer accept proposals unless they have personally requested, or "solicited" one.

This extreme competition coupled with the lack of personal contact makes grant writing a long shot. As I mentioned earlier, a typical expectation is that only ten percent of the proposals you write will be funded, and this assumes excellent, thorough writing and grant research that ensures all of these perfect proposals went to likely funders.

By the way, if you are lucky enough to personally know a decision maker at a foundation, approach them following the direct ask concepts

I described earlier in this chapter. With this personal connection, such a grant proposal becomes that ideal person-to-person connection. But, once this person gives you the thumbs up to submit a proposal, you will still need to follow the foundation's proposal guidelines exactly because your buddy is likely not the only person to review it.

While I caution against high expectations for grants, I still recommend including grant writing in your fundraising activities. But first learn the common procedures of grant writing from books and local workshops. Also, talk with grant writing experts in your community to get a full picture of this process. Then, do all the preliminary work necessary to ensure you find the grantors who are most likely to fund your organization.

Find potential foundations through nonprofit associations that serve your region. In the U.S., The Foundation Center www.foundationcenter.org is a good start. Your local library may also offer a grant research service. Another great way to find likely grantors is to check the list of supporters on the websites of organizations that are similar to yours.

Once you've found them, follow every detail in their grant instructions! Use their same headings for each section so they can easily find the information they expect. Use specifics just as with any other funder such as the number of people you expect to serve in your first year.

In the U.S., a great resource for numbers of people living in poverty is www.City-Data.com. There you'll find census data broken out for cities and even neighborhoods. They sort the data to make it easy to pull out clear numbers you can use in your proposals to show the need and how many people will be served by the grant. If you don't find exactly what you need at City-Data, check the main U.S. Census site: www.census.gov. That site is more difficult to use, but with enough patience you'll find what you need.

For worldwide data on poverty and disadvantaged people, check:

- World Bank's data site: data.worldbank.org/
- World Health Organization (WHO): www.who.int/en

You can also search the web for poverty statistics in your country. But beware of websites that embellish data for their own benefit. Some international charity sites tend to bend the measurements of poverty, inflating the numbers in order to raise more money. Don't ever fall into this damaging habit. As a local organization the risk of harming your reputation is high and simply not worth it. Check all your data sources and only use numbers that are backed up by other sources and that align with what you have experienced in your community. Also beware of data sources that use strange measures. For instance, in rural areas where people own their houses and can live quite comfortably off the land they own, measuring poverty by a dollar amount earned per day does not work. Expect funders who are familiar with your area to know such discrepancies.

Look beyond poverty figures as well. Depending on your community there could be several different groups of disadvantaged and marginalized people. Such marginalization often leads to poverty, but understanding these root causes will help you create a more effective program that also remedies these causes before they do harm to people. Prejudice and racism are some of the most obvious. But even they can be elusive. Consider all sorts of people in your community who are struggling and ending up in poverty. Don't forget seniors, teenagers and disabled people. Look at your culture and honestly assess if certain people are judged differently simply because of their race, skin color, sex, age or ability. Then show this awareness and need in your proposals through broader demographics data. Clearly connect your program's goals with poverty alleviation e.g., how much time and money the bicycles you provide will save people, the job opportunities your program will create with their funding, and so on.

Besides making the case for your program using demographics data, make sure your proposal budget lines up. The worst blunder you can make is to leave out a zero or add up columns incorrectly. Funders often look at a budget first because it is a clear snapshot of what the proposal is requesting from them. If a budget is sloppy or incorrect, they will likely reject the proposal before reading on. So spend quality time creating your budget to align with your proposal and give it one last careful look before you submit it.

Once you and your team are ready to begin the arduous process of grant writing, create two important tools that will save you time in the years to come:

1. Grant proposal template: Most grantors ask for similar sections of information including: proposal summary, about your organization, the need, intended outcomes, methods, evaluation, and budget. Creating a template with all the common information that you will repeat for every proposal will save lots of time.

2. Spreadsheet of funders and potential funders: Here you can record the foundations you discover in your research on the web, through supporters lists at like-minded organizations, and tips from friends. Be sure to highlight their proposal deadlines. At first, it will only have one sheet of potential funders, but later you can add sheets for "submitted" and "upcoming." You might also want a sheet that captures foundations that appeared to be a good fit but are not so you don't waste time looking at them again. And just as with all funders, you will want to return to the foundations that funded your organization to request their support again.

Government grants are a whole different ballgame from foundation grants. They are also a long shot for small organizations. Government agencies prefer to work with large, well established organizations. Still, they might seem to be a good fit for launching your program. Just remember that they require tedious registrations, forms and processes meaning that years can pass before approval. National government grant programs usually require the organization to have an annual audit of its finances by an outside accountant, a costly and time consuming process. Local government grants are somewhat easier. If you are already using an annual audit process and are willing to grind through the mounds of forms and requirements, government grants can be excellent long-term funding sources. I've found that once a government agency trusts a nonprofit and is happy with its work, they are likely to continue funding that program with only a minor amount of renewal procedure required. If you think you're ready to apply for a government grant, look at their funding programs in the areas of affordable transportation and jobs creation.

Government grants differ from government contracts. Just like any grant, a government grant provides one payment to accomplish a finite goal. In contrast, a government contract, just like any contract, is a business agreement for your organization to carryout a job for them. Government contracts are not appropriate for raising capital to launch your program because they require programs to be underway in order to demonstrate that they fit the particular job that government agency needs performed. I will discuss some potentials for government contracts in Chapter 12.

Indirect Asks

There are many methods of asking for donations indirectly—mass mailings, emails, press releases, website appeals, online fundraising challenges through other sites, Facebook and other social media. None of these will bring in the significant funding you will need to launch your program because they lack the direct connection of people giving to people. However, don't skip these. Make them a constant backdrop of your capital fundraising effort that promotes your organization's need. Not only will these bring in small donations that add to the total, they can also reach your potential major donors, sponsors and grantors before you approach them, familiarizing them with your capital fundraising effort and adding to their confidence to give.

To increase your chances of success with mailings and email appeals, spend quality time building and updating the list of people you will send it to as I described in Chapter 2.

One final note on ensuring the success of your capital fundraising efforts: Get your entire leadership team involved. Some might enjoy the backstage work like compiling the list of potential donors or grant research. Others might be more social and enjoy event planning. Just be sure that every one of your fellow leaders takes on an important role in this fundraising effort. Not only are the core leaders of any organization the best at inspiring others to give, donors will recognize and appreciate this commitment from the leaders.

And don't forget to have fun. Raising funds to launch such an important program should be an industrious and enjoyable venture. Your enthusiasm to succeed will spread to your fellow leaders and on to donors who will be anxious to see their donation come to fruition. With such a spirit to succeed, you'll have the capital you need to launch your program before you know it. So read on to the next section to take a look at what your program might be like once it is in motion.

Section 2

Your Program in Motion

CHAPTER 6

Launching Your Program

The planning and fundraising work you've done to prepare for the launch of your program will have revealed important details about your best first steps. However, until all of you are at the brink of the launch, you won't know exactly how it will look. In fact, the planning and fundraising stage can give false impressions of grandeur. In order to fully plan your program, all of you must think big. And in order to demonstrate the long-term potential of your program, your funding requests must show significant impact. But what does that first week really look like?

The reality of today is always less glamorous than long-term planning. This is a good thing and something all of you will need to accept. Otherwise, you could launch your program with too many promises and set up your clients, funders and partners for disappointment. Be sure to differentiate between those long-term goals and the reality of the launch even during the planning process. Let everyone know there will be lots of work to do before you reach those goals and that you need them to stick with you through the bumpy grind of the launch.

There are two ways to launch a Social Bike Business program:

1. With the grand opening of your bicycle community center (this can include the renovation of the same building you've occupied prior to taking on the program);
2. Without your bicycle community center.

Of course, the first option is the most spectacular and the best for capturing media attention. If you and your team are fortunate enough to have a building ready to open when you launch your program, you will be able to ramp up your program in the most direct manner. Such a building might be completely donated to your organization or leased at a very low rate, perhaps even one dollar a year. In either case, get all the details of the donation or lease in writing and have your pro bono attorney check the details before you sign.

You might also have a chance at receiving a low interest loan that will allow your organization to purchase a building over time. Only an organization that is well established with most of the systems described in this book in place should even consider taking on such a major loan. But if you and your team are comfortable with this concept, it's worth checking into. In the U.S., local community development corporations (CDC) manage property loans that attract businesses to distressed neighborhoods. With enough capacity and a great sales pitch, your organization could qualify. Do a web search for "community development corporation" or "certified development corporation" for your area.

By having your building ready to go at launch, you will see how the rooms work, test the uses and make adjustments as your early clients begin to take part. This is a big advantage. Budget for all the likely expenses, pay all the fees and have all the registrations and approvals in place that are required by your local government before moving ahead with your launch. These will likely include:

- Business license
- Business name registration (using the same name as your organization avoids extra paperwork)
- Zoning qualifications
- Fire inspection
- Sign permit
- Certificate of occupancy
- Liability insurance
- Sellers permit and sales tax registration
- Utility deposits and upgrades to bring building up to code (work with a city inspector well in advance to find out the required upgrades and costs)

This is by no means a complete list. Check with your local, state and national governments to be sure you have everything in place before you open. Otherwise you could face heavy fines. Your pro bono accountant and local small business association can also help you find and prepare for all the required permits.

Very few of our local partners are lucky enough to secure a perfect building for their center before they are ready to move ahead with their program. That's okay. There is no limit to the combinations of options you can look at for launching without your own building. Here are just a few:

- Rent a building that is not ideal, but will work in the short term (this will still come with all the local business opening requirements mentioned above),

- Partner with a vocational school or other job training facility where you can hold your career training classes,
- Refurbish donated bikes and develop your micro lending system in a non-public place such as a home office then schedule career training classes and/or bicycle presentations every few weeks at a large facility that can accommodate many clients and helpers.

Obviously, such options are not ideal, so I encourage you and your team to do everything you can to obtain your own building before you launch your program. But if that is simply not possible, get creative, work with your partners and make it work. Sometimes launching your program without a building will be the best way to demonstrate your organization's commitment to the program and show funders and even potential building donors how much you need your own building.

The other big decisions you and your team will have to make are the actual first steps that will best serve your long-term goals. Carefully consider all the potential first steps you could succeed with, then look at how each will set your organization up for long-term success. For instance, if you do not have your own building yet, but you do have lots of free, covered and secure storage available, launching your program with a call for bicycle donations could be a great first step. This call for bikes would be an excellent promotional vehicle for the launch of your program and would offer lots of people an easy way to get involved by donating a bike they no longer need.

However, if you do not have ample covered and secure storage to receive potentially hundreds of donated bikes, these donors will find out that you had to store them outside or at lots of different locations. This will appear terribly unprofessional and undermine your organization's reputation for many years to come.

The same concern could play out for launching your program with career training. If you schedule and promote bicycle career training classes for disadvantaged people, but when they show up, you are not prepared to teach these courses through to the end, they will quickly spread the word that your organization is not to be bothered with. So choose your first steps for launching your program very carefully.

Another important consideration is the culture of your organization and community. Will career training resonate best with the people who care about your organization or would they rather see and touch bicycles? Even if career training seems logically best, if the culture of the people you are working with points to bicycles, give this serious thought. Fueling the passion of the people who engage in and are important to your program is very important. Their passion to help and spread the word about your program is a significant long-term asset.

Examples of Social Bike Business Program Launches
RIDE 4 A WOMAN (R4W)

Ride 4 a Woman's mission is to empower the local impoverished women with bicycles. Ugandan culture prevents women from riding bicycles or repairing anything. Their Social Bike Business program is designed to break this taboo and thus open up career opportunities to local women as well as provide them with bicycles. R4W is based in Buhoma, Uganda right next to the world-renowned Bwindi Impenetrable Forest where the last mountain gorillas live. Many tourists visit the region every year to see the gorillas. So R4W's leaders realized that they could rent bicycles to these tourists to generate the income they needed to build their Women's Community Centre. This centre is where they offer their women members career training classes, not just in bicycle repair, but in crafts making and tailoring.

Soon after R4W was founded in 2009, they received a long-term very affordable lease of land where they could build their centre. At the same time, they received some early donations to purchase their first mountain bikes to rent to tourists. These early breakthroughs pointed clearly to two first steps they used to launch their program. They unveiled the bikes in an attractive bike rental stand by the park entrance with lots of promotion to encourage the tourists to rent them. At the same time, they called their women members together to begin the construction of their centre.

By combining these two rather different first steps, they clearly showed how these two parts of their program aligned. The tourists could see how their renting of R4W's bikes was helping local women. And by gathering the women to begin construction, including using the very first bike rental money for materials, their members could clearly see how R4W's bike rentals would benefit them.

Read more on R4W's website: www.ride4awoman.org.

SOCIAL BIKE BUSINESS BUDAPEST

The leadership team for this program is made up of leaders from many partner organizations. The lead organization is called ZöFi, or the Hungarian Green Roots. ZöFi is a strong organization with a cozy office in Budapest's most distressed neighborhood, the Eighth District. This location is perfect for a Social Bike Business program, but their office is nowhere near large enough to house the program. Other partners have excellent connections with city government and neighborhood organizations that often donate abandoned buildings to programs like Social Bike Business Budapest. But try as they have, no usable building could be found by the time they were ready to launch their program.

Another important factor in their choice of first steps was that Hungary has a very comprehensive state career training certification program. These certifications are highly regarded by employers and citizens alike. In fact, there was already a bicycle mechanic certification curriculum available and endorsed by the state.

Without a building to start with, but with many partner organizations eager to help with career training, including a funding sponsor, the leadership team made the choice to launch their program with their first class of 15 impoverished people eager to become bicycle mechanics. They held the academic classes at ZöFi's office and provided the hands-on training at a supportive local vocational school. All 15 graduated in May of 2011. This success and the stories from these students are now the substance of grant proposals and donor requests, including their continued search for a donated building for their center. Soon after their first class graduated, they received an invitation from NESsT, an international nonprofit that supports social enterprises, to participate in their business plan assistance program. They have also begun work on their own certification training that will fit their program for the long term.

By accepting that a building could not be found right away and by listening to the local cultural passion for career training, Budapest's leadership team launched their program with a reasonable first step that is helping them build their program toward success.

Read more on their program web page: www.zofi.hu/projektek/socialbike.

Tapping the Launch for Great Promotions
The launch of your program is one of the best promotional opportunities you will have, so make the most of it. Whether it's a ribbon cutting at the opening of your center or a day of celebration with bike donations, make sure you draw a crowd that includes the media and prominent officials. These officials and reporters will take pride in having attended your opening event and this will endear them to your program, making them easier to approach for assistance in the future.

In order to create an opening event that attracts such key people, you and your team will have to plan this special day well in advance. In the previous chapter, I went over the significant amount of time needed to plan a successful fundraising event. A launch day celebration won't need quite as much lead time, but I recommend starting the planning at least three months ahead of the date. This will give you and your team enough time to flesh out your plans for the day, create fun graphics and materials, and then begin the invitations to your officials, media connections and all of your supporters.

If you can give your officials some time to speak at the event, this will provide two important benefits: they are more likely to attend and they will have to learn important details about your program to include in their speech. If you've allowed enough lead time, you can get their commitment to attend and then include this in your press release about the event. Send your press release to all the newspapers, radio and TV stations in your area at least two weeks prior to your event. Then follow up with phone calls to personally invite reporters to attend.

You can make your launch day event lots of fun with all sorts of activities. Consider a bicycle theater or bike games. In your promotions, you could announce a competition in bike art or other talents and have attendees pick the winners at the event. Invite people to create temporary sculptures or chalk drawings on the pavement. Let your imaginations run wild.

With all these possibilities popping, I need to return to the concept of fundraising events and their similarity to an opening event in order to ask an important question: Why not make your opening event a fundraising event, too? While there are many reasons why not to that all fall into the category of extra work, the reasons for expanding the event are quite compelling, mostly in the extra money category. If you and your team believe you have the time, energy and resources to succeed with such a major event at the very start of your program, by all means give it a go. But remember, you'll have to at least double your lead time to six months if not a year. Also be sure to fully study the type of fundraising event you'd like to create and bring in an expert to lead it. Even if you decide not to expand it to a full fundraising event, be sure to ask for donations at the opening. This sets that long-term precedent of constant fundraising.

The most important aspect of organizing a great event for your program's launch is promotion. So don't hold back! Tap every possible promotion potential you and your helpers can dream up. Here are the absolutes, but have fun adding to this list with many more creative ideas:

- **Website:** Refresh your website and splash the launch event date, time and activities all over the home page (see Chapter 4 for website basics),
- **E-news:** If you haven't yet created an e-newsletter, this would be the time to do it. There are lots of e-newsletter services available—some free, others that charge a fee—but all require time to set up. The easiest way to go, at least at the start, is to create a nice html template that looks good when emailed, leave the middle blank for text, type up the details of your event and send it bcc to all the emails you've collected from your list of helpers. Even from the start, include instructions on how to unsubscribe from future e-newsletters for those who are not interested.
- **Social media:** Condense your event details into the basics and post it to Facebook, Twitter, and all the other social media sites you and your team are connected to. Definitely create a separate event page on Facebook and post that around as well. Include a request for folks to forward it on. And always include a link to your website. Never consider social media sites to be

the final destination. They need to direct people to your website where they can learn more about your program, get involved and perhaps even donate.

- **Flyers & word of mouth:** Put up flyers around your neighborhood and ask neighborhood leaders to spread the word. You want to ensure that the disadvantaged people your program means to serve feel welcome to attend the opening event.

The most important thing to remember about your launch day event is that it is only the *start* of all of your program's promotions. Repeat and build on all of the promotion methods you use for your event from that point on. Do not consider it an isolated or separate promotion opportunity. Just as you want your officials and reporters to attend so that you can begin building a long-term relationship with them, view all the people you connect with in the same way. Many people will see your e-news, flyers and website, but only a fraction of them will attend the event. Make sure that all of your messaging and materials inspire these people to get involved for the long term whether or not they attend. Add promotion activities to your work plan each year, including at least three press releases to your local media agencies about success stories and upcoming events.

At the launch event, include various ways everyone can get involved. Have a helper offering a program sign up sheet throughout the event so people who need a bike or career training can easily sign up. Have another sign up sheet for eager volunteers and/or donors that captures their post and email addresses. Add all of these to your list of helpers.

Think of your launch day event as a springboard into your program that can give it an enormous boost as it inspires all sorts of people to take part in its success.

Next we'll look at the daily considerations of running your program to ensure it does the best job possible of serving the bicycle needs of disadvantaged people.

CHAPTER 7

Serving the Bicycle Needs of Disadvantaged People

When I discuss the Social Bike Business program with people they often ask me what I mean by "disadvantaged." Some express suspicion, concerned that ineligible people will abuse the program. Others clearly have no idea. Oddly, when I mention the term "poor" I usually get a nod of understanding. But speaking only of poverty misses the point of this program. In order to fully embrace what Social Bike Business can do for people and the world, you've got to see the spectrum of struggles that disadvantaged people face. Consider young people tempted by gangs; people shut out of society for a characteristic they have no power to change; seniors, disabled people and anyone who has come to believe they are no longer a valued part of their community. Poverty is a common result of such shunning, but it is not the root cause.

As a leader of your own Social Bike Business program it is up to you to peer deeply into your community, to ask the tough questions and discover the people who have been pushed to the fringe. Don't be tempted to describe only poverty. Listen for the prejudice from those who shun and listen for the anger from those who have been shunned. Until you find the most disadvantaged, marginalized people in your community, you won't know the people your program is designed to help. Here are a few examples from our local partners around the world:

- In Uganda, the leaders of Ride 4 a Woman discovered that women were the most disadvantaged in their area due to the taboo against them driving vehicles, repairing anything or having a career.
- In India, the leaders of Rickshaw Bank discovered that rickshaw drivers were oppressed by rickshaw owners who fed them addictive drugs and stole nearly all the money they earned.

- In Budapest, the leaders of Social Bike Business Budapest knew all too well that the Roma people (derogatorily called "gypsies") had been persecuted, enslaved and murdered for hundreds of years.

Once each of these leadership teams zeroed in on the most marginalized group in their community, they had their gauge for success. Each day they could measure the success of their program simply by looking to see if any from their most disadvantaged group were participating. If not, they knew they had to make changes to better reach out to this group and make them feel more welcome.

As I explained in Chapter 1, success with the Social Bike Business program is measured by a single bottom line: the number of disadvantaged people served by the program. Your community may have several different disadvantaged groups so simply look to ensure that some from any of these groups are participating at all times. This single bottom line includes the monetary bottom line by default because profits are necessary in order to serve as many of these people as possible. To further refine and make use of this bottom line of number of disadvantaged people served we could change it to *most* disadvantaged. Only by seeking out and serving the most disadvantaged people in your community will you open the doors of your center to your entire community. And simply by prioritizing those who have been shunned by others, your program will dismantle the barriers between the shunned and those who have shunned them.

Learning the Needs of Disadvantaged People

In order to learn what your community's disadvantaged people need, you have to ask them. This is more difficult than it may seem. People who have been shunned by society have lost trust in anyone who is not in their immediate circle of friends and family. Well meaning charity and government programs have taught them how to answer to thoughtless questions in order to get a handout. Such fabricated answers are far from what you need to learn in order to do a great job serving their needs with your program

So you need to start by building trust. One of the best ways to do so is to find a neighborhood leader who is willing to discuss the program with you. This person can then vouch for you and encourage others to talk with you. You'll want to find out the answers to such questions as:

- Do they need bikes or do they already have bikes that simply need to be repaired?
- What sort of bicycling would ease their transportation burden? Do they need to ride long distance or simply to a bus or train?
- What sort of loads do they need to carry? Does this include children?
- If they could choose a career, what would it be?

- Do they need help finding a job?
- Would they like to own their own business? What sort?

You and your team will come up with other questions depending on your community and the people you aim to serve with your program. The important thing is to *ask* and then *listen*.

Through One Street's local partners for the program we have found some clear patterns. Regarding the bicycles to be refurbished and manufactured by local programs, the need for sturdy and durable transportation bicycles that impoverished people can purchase is loud and clear in every community I've connected with. This means that weight is not as important as the bicycle's durability. Performance is also not as important as function. For instance, smooth shifting that hits each gear perfectly is not as important as a shifting system that will function well for many years of hard use.

Listen also for where and how the bicycles will be used. You might live in a city with hills, but if your marginalized neighbors mainly travel in the flat areas of the city, five or even one gear could be plenty. This would allow you a wider range of refurbished bikes to offer and help you design a more affordable bike once you are ready to manufacture. The same goes for wheel and tire sizes. If folks need to travel long distances, a larger wheel size like 27 or 28 inches with narrower tires will be the most efficient. But if there are lots of hills and roads are rough, the 26 inch mountain bike wheel size with the wider tires will give them more control and handling over rough areas. But make sure to *ask*!

For the design of your manufactured bicycles, they must include racks and/or baskets for carrying large loads and children (sometimes these can be added to refurbished bikes as well). This means that the wheelbase should be longer than recreational bikes in order to add stability for the rider. This leads to a great example of why asking your local disadvantaged people is so important. When One Street started our program and I heard these cries for load carrying capabilities, I began to envision the same social bike design for all our partners with built-in racks and a very long wheelbase. But, because I was asking and listening, I learned that in some communities people need bikes that can be loaded onto bus racks or carried on trains. Others, like in New York City, have to carry their bikes up narrow stairways to secure them in their apartments. That's when I knew that each community we work with will have to design their own social bike, and in order to do so, the leaders of the local program will have to listen carefully to the needs of their neighbors. Early in your program, before you are ready to manufacture your own bicycles,

this deep understanding will help you turn away types of donated bikes that are low priority if your storage space is limited. If you have ample covered and secure storage, you could accept all bikes and let the donors know that inappropriate bikes will likely be torn down for parts and recycling or sold to generate funds.

Career training is no less dependent on understanding the needs of the people you aim to serve. As you will see in the next chapter, there are many angles you can take in the career training program. For instance, if most people want to own their own social bike shop, you will want to promote and encourage the whole certification program. But if most are interested in owning different types of businesses such as mobile bicycle vendors to serve a tourist area, you could lead off with the business management module. The same could go for customer service in a big city where people are interested in jobs at large retailers. In that case you could lead off with the customer service module.

Also consider offering a job search service by reaching out to employers in your community. When a great candidate for a job comes to you, you can champion them to these employers and offer to help prepare the new employee for the job.

The most important thing to remember is that you must *listen*. This is not easy because each of us is far more interested in our own voice than in others. As a leader, you will also be tempted to believe that you know more than other people. This may be true, but when it comes to designing your program, remember that the information you know is nowhere near as important as the information you must glean from your disadvantaged neighbors.

Once you have established their trust, find a place and a time that allows them to relax. Use a notepad to capture their ideas. Taking notes is an excellent way to show respect in any meeting. When people have spent their lives being shunned, every effort you make to show respect will resonate with them.

Taking notes is just one way to show you are listening. Also sit forward, not slouched back. Briefly respond to interesting ideas they offer. When it's time for you to speak again, repeat part of what they said in your own words and ask them if you are capturing their meaning.

Use their language. This might seem obvious, especially if they speak a totally different language than yours, in which case you might also need an interpreter. But what I actually mean by this is to speak in a way they are sure to understand. If you have spent most of your life with advantaged people or worse, in academic settings, realize that the way you speak will not only be off-putting to someone who lives on the edge of society, they may not even understand you. Before such meetings, practice your choice in words. Listen to these marginalized people as they communicate with each other. If you're about to use a word they may not understand, slow down and search for a better, more respectful way of communicating what you need to say.

In order to do a good job of listening, be sure they spend more time speaking than you. With people who are not used to such respect, this can be difficult. The best method I've found is to offer more questions than statements. Remember, their expertise is far more important than yours and the only way you can learn from them is to encourage them to talk. Questions will open this communication channel so you can listen and learn from these valuable experts.

Making Your Center Welcoming to Disadvantaged People

Whether you launch your program with or without your bicycle community center, eventually you will open your center and it is vital that it welcomes your disadvantaged neighbors. As I mentioned in Chapter 4, a location in a distressed neighborhood that is easily accessed on foot and bike by most of the disadvantaged people in the community and easy to access from the street for pedestrians, bicyclists and drivers is very important. A welcoming, professional storefront and outside seating will also draw people to your site.

However, just making your center easy to approach isn't enough. People have to want to come in and stay once they are inside. A glass front door or big glass windows will let newcomers see inside and show them they can enter and exit easily. Fear of entrapment applies to all retail customers, but far more to impoverished people who are victimized more than others. Even if you have to open your center before your classrooms and repair area are ready, be sure that your welcome area is fully equipped, clean and ready to welcome your clients. Staff it with a caring person who lives in the neighborhood and can sign them up for a bike and career training. Also train this person in basic bike repair so they can check over bikes and let the owners know of any repairs needed to make their bike safe for riding.

Providing Bicycles, Parts and Repair Service

Refurbished bikes will likely be your best way to provide bicycles at the start. As I've already mentioned, this is not as easy as it might seem. Most of our local partners who are already engaged in refurbishing bikes tell us that as few as ten percent of the bicycles they receive as donations are good enough quality and in good enough shape to refurbish. Remember, yours is not a charity bike giveaway program. You're creating a professional, business-oriented program that will *sell* quality bikes to people who need them the most. Later in this chapter I'll discuss micro loans and subsidies that will allow the poorest person to buy a bike. No matter how much they end up paying out of pocket, these are your customers and you have to provide them with a safe, quality bike that fits their needs and will last them a long time. This means that all the donated bikes that cannot be refurbished to this high standard must be stripped down, parts sorted and the rest recycled immediately or they will fill your storage. Even so, once you make the call for donated bicycles for your refurbishing program, you will be buried in bikes, ninety percent of which will require significant time to break down and dispose of.

On a similar note, pull out bikes that are made for only sport riding because they will be useless for your clients. Any front or rear suspension will be a detriment because even quality suspension systems breakdown within one year and are very expensive to repair. Remove front suspension forks and replace them with rigid forks, and never provide a bike with rear suspension to a client. Fancy road racing bikes are similarly useless to disadvantaged people because they cannot carry loads and they are very unstable. However, such fancy bikes can bring a premium if you can sell them to retail customers. They are also fabulous auction items if you decide to try your hand at fundraising events. Make sure you record the name and contact info of the owner of any fancy bike that is donated. Fancy sport bikes are often the target of thieves. One of these thieves might think they are doing a lovely community service by donating a hot bike, but you could end up having to do a lot of explaining to the police if the original owner shows up. This would also be damaging to your organization's reputation.

Because of this expected deluge of bikes, your top priority must be ample covered and secure storage. I estimate that five hundred square feet is the minimum you'll need just for the storage of these bikes. On top of that, you will also need another five hundred square feet for tearing down unusable bikes and sorting the parts. If you can create a separate or at least mobile repair station just for this storage and sorting area, that will prevent this chaotic process from disrupting the repair area used for customers and clients. A mobile repair station can be rolled outside of the storage area for tearing down bikes, then rolled back in for secure storage.

The next priority in any bicycle refurbishing program is a system for ensuring each bike receives a thorough safety check before it goes to a client or is sold at retail. Find an example of a safety checklist in Appendix B. This safety check must be done by an experienced bicycle mechanic, so at the start of your program you'll need to employ such a mechanic for this service. Once your career training is underway, graduates of your advanced repair module will qualify for this position. In Chapter 9, I'll discuss insurance, but for now realize that selling an unsafe bicycle opens your organization up for major liability. This is another drawback of refurbished bikes—they need far more scrutiny than new bikes because their frame, fork and every part needs to be checked for excessive wear, cracks or damage.

In order to service your donated bikes that can be refurbished as well as client bikes, you will need to set up an account with a wholesale bicycle parts distributor. Any legitimate wholesaler will require you to have a professional storefront and business license. These applications are quite thorough and generally take some time to process before you are approved for your first order, so get started on this as soon as your center is open and operational. If you have a nice relationship with a bike shop owner in your town, this person can help you sort through this process and could even help you prioritize your early orders. If you have been working with One Street to develop your program, our recommendation of your organization to a wholesale distributor could also assist this process.

The Social Bike Business program does not include imported new bicycles because bicycles manufactured overseas usually come from abusive factories. These factories pay very low wages, force their employees to work long hours, and the bicycles produced there do not benefit those communities. These abuses undermine the program's bottom line of serving as many disadvantaged people as possible. So, while your wholesale distributor might provide new bikes, I highly discourage you from filling your welcome area floor with them. However, if a client is desperate for a bicycle, these undesirable bikes can take care of urgencies as long as you and your team understand the negative social effect of purchasing such bicycles and avoid it except for urgencies.

In Chapter 11 I'll discuss the details of manufacturing your own bicycles. At the start of your program, if manufacturing is something you want to add, the main consideration is to ensure you are setting the stage for this advanced step in your program. Most importantly, set aside ample room for manufacturing at your center. Situate this area at the back or to the side of your center so it can have its own service entry where raw materials can be delivered without disrupting the center's welcome area or classes.

Bicycle repair is another important service you and your team will have to provide from the start of your program. Even if you launch your program without your center open, safety checks of the bicycles already owned by disadvantaged people will be a primary service you must offer. Many bicycle crashes are caused by poor maintenance including loose wheels, poorly adjusted brakes, low tire pressure, and other easily fixed problems.

At your center, your bicycle repair and service area will be a focal point, not only for safety repairs for clients, but for service to retail customers. Work with an experienced bicycle mechanic to set up your service area with professional bike repair stands, easy-to-reach professional bicycle tools and common repair parts. This mechanic can help you prioritize your first tool purchases to ensure you spend your money on necessities first. You don't want to open your repair area with all the latest wheel building equipment yet not have the tools to adjust brakes and gears. Once you have enough funds to stock two or more repair stations, create a separate repair and service station for your training program so that classes do not disrupt your professional bicycle repair service for your daily customers and clients.

Encouraging Clients to Engage with Your Program

You might think that all you need to do is open your center and your most disadvantaged neighbors will flock to your program. Unfortunately, this is generally not the case. You're going to have to work hard at catching their attention and then convincing them to take part.

Understanding the common communication methods these folks use will help you choose the best means for connecting with them. From what I've learned from our local partners in different communities around the world, there are three areas of communication you and your team will have to fully develop in order to connect.

1) <u>Refine your program message</u> so that everyone involved in your program can say it in ten seconds or less. This message must focus on the benefits to the person it addresses, use their language, be void of anything that might be threatening to a marginalized person, and be compelling enough to entice them to act. Compare these examples:

"The Social Bike Business program has been extensively reviewed in order to serve the needs of the poor through comprehensive program development and planning with key stakeholders. You would be advised to sign up at (address)."

"I've been helping create (insert the name of your program) and we're finally able to offer transportation bicycles and job training to people who are ready for them. Are you interested in getting your own bike or starting your own business?"

Both examples fit the ten second rule, but only one has even the faintest chance of engaging folks in the program. Include yourself in your message so they know that you are committed to being their personal connection to the program. Practice your messaging to ensure it is free of jargon and threatening academic language. Once you and your team are happy with it, be sure that everyone you ask to promote your program understands the difference and can articulate the benefits of your program in a nonthreatening manner.

2) <u>Create written material</u> that follows the above principles and is short and concise. Such a one page handout or tri-fold brochure will give your helpers a way to invite people to the program without seeming to force them to decide right then. Your helpers, whether out in the community or at your center, can introduce the program with your agreed-upon message and then give the person this handout to consider.

3) <u>Word of mouth</u> will follow any success you have with the first two above. You can also encourage word of mouth by asking your first clients to tell their friends. If they had a positive experience with your program, they are going to be the very best ambassadors you could ever dream of. But don't expect them to remember to spread the good word

about your program. As I noted before, people are twelve times more likely to spread the word about a bad experience than they are about a good one. A simple prompt will help them remember.

Setting up Your Micro Lending and Subsidy Program

There is no denying the benefits of a micro loan for someone who has no savings. With a very small loan they can manage to purchase a bike. With a larger loan they can open their own social bike shop.

Micro lending, also known as microfinance, was pioneered in the 1970s by Grameen Bank in Bangladesh. They provided small loans to help people start their own businesses. This allowed each new business owner to buy materials, sell the products they made with the materials, and pay back their loan with the money they earned. More than ninety percent of these loans were fully paid off within the allotted time. In order to cover all the costs of serving many small loans, interests are higher than other loans, usually around twenty percent for reputable organizations. Since Grameen's success in those early years, many other nonprofits, government agencies and for-profit lending institutions have replicated this concept.

However, the results of micro lending have not been so rosy. In areas served by micro lending organizations poverty has not been reduced significantly. Speculators point to the high interest rates as the reason for this. They also point to the people who fail to pay back their loans or spend far too long paying them back, incurring untold expense in interest and shame from their neighbors, and finding themselves deeper in poverty. I suspect that the reason for these unspectacular results is broader. No loan can remedy the many pervasive causes of poverty. These are important reminders—micro loans cannot cure poverty and they come with risks just like any other debt.

An even more serious concern is that abusive nonprofits and lending companies have learned that they can reap millions more dollars through micro loans by raising their interest rates and tacking on hidden fees. These large, often international organizations and companies work hard to hide their abusive tactics.

A recent example of lending abuse from large institutions occurred in the U.S. with the home lending crisis. Millions of homes are now in foreclosure because lenders cared more about profit than their clients' wellbeing.

More brazen examples are the street corner check cashing and money lending shops. They often refer to their loan services as micro lending, likely to tap the warm, charity appeal of this term. These predatory lending sharks set up shop in distressed neighborhoods and draw their "customers" in with the lure of easy money. They require borrowers to put up whatever property they own as collateral, sometimes a house or a car. But their interest and hidden fees are so high many borrowers cannot repay the loan and even if they do, they lose more money in interest and fees than they borrowed. Such lenders happily take their clients' money and collateral and spit them back out into deeper poverty.

Predatory lending practices have given micro lending a bad name. If you choose to add it to your program, distance your organization from any predatory lenders in your community and make sure your clients know that your organization does not operate that way.

A smaller threat, but certainly a potential distraction, comes from the many flaky organizations that claim to offer micro loans. These, much like the predatory lenders, have multiplied in response to all the promotion and media surrounding micro lending in the past twenty or so years. In my research on micro lending I have found far more well-meaning worthless flakes than I have reputable professional micro lenders. So don't be distracted by pretty websites. Make sure they have satisfied clients to prove their worth.

The best way to add microfinance to your program is to partner with a local, reputable nonprofit, bank or credit union that already has a lending system in place. Avoid large banks and international organizations because they can never place your clients' interest as primary.

If you and your team choose to administer the loans through your organization, start with your accountant and attorney to ensure you meet all of your government's requirements for providing loans. If there is any significant result from the proliferation of predatory lenders, besides increased poverty, it's an equal proliferation of government regulations. So be prepared for this. In the U.S., you can find many requirements through the Federal Trade Commission at www.ftc.gov. Connect with reputable micro lenders in your area to learn from their experience. Also, charge enough interest to cover your administration costs even as you set up your system to be as affordable and achievable as possible for your clients.

Below are some examples of reputable micro lending organizations. They all require local programs to become partners before assisting them, but you can likely find pertinent resources on their websites and they may even answer simple questions if you email or call them.

- ACCION www.accion.org
- Grameen (find your local chapter)
- Kiva www.kiva.org
- U.S. Small Business Administration microloan program - for social bike shops www.sba.gov/content/microloan-program

Set up your subsidy program at the same time you set up your micro loan program. It will become an important part of your fundraising efforts allowing donors and grantors to provide specific funds to your organization to offset the cost of a bicycle for your most impoverished clients. You'll learn your clients' level of need during the qualifying process, which I discuss below. Work with your team to determine the criteria that will make this process fair. But even if you manage to raise enough funds to cover the entire retail price of the bikes these folks need, don't let them have them for free! Even if they have to pay with their last ten dollars, this will instill a value for their new bike. I've lost count of how many bike program leaders I've discussed this with who have learned the hard way not to give away bikes. Something that comes free will never be fully valued. Free bikes are left out in the rain, run into the ground without any maintenance, and traded for stupid things.

Qualifying Individuals for Your Program Services

Many of the program services you offer at your center will be tailored to the needs of disadvantaged people. For instance, people who are living in poverty do not have any spare money to use for buying a bike and certainly not enough to start their own business. Your subsidy and micro loan programs can help them achieve these goals. Also, your career training program must charge fees that cover all costs associated with the training, but disadvantaged clients, the very people you want in these trainings, will not have the money available to pay for these fees. You might also set up micro lending and subsidy systems to help struggling people pay for repairs to bikes they already own and purchase parts and accessories they need. Such assistance will look mighty tempting for swindlers who are not actually disadvantaged, but want to get your products and services at a reduced rate or through a loan. Not only would such misuse of funds waste the limited, hard-won grants and donations you raised for this purpose, it would undermine your program's reputation.

In order to ensure only disadvantaged people can tap into your program you must set in place a multi-level system of qualifying each individual that applies for your program's assistance. Start with a thorough application process that requires them to fill out an extensive form and then, a few days later, meet with one of your staff to explain their reason for their need. If what they wrote in the application does not match what they tell your staff member, this could be a red flag. But don't disqualify them until you are sure they are lying.

Next, they must produce some documentation that proves they

are living in poverty. In most countries this can include social services documentation they might receive for food or housing assistance.

Also consider seeking out a neighborhood champion who is known and trusted by at least one person on your team and who also knows and can vouch for the applicant. This neighborhood champion can point out meager living conditions, lack of a bike or other means of transportation, that they've seen the individual in line for social services, and other details that point to their need. On the other hand, this champion might reveal that the person owns their own house, has a fancy car, owns several other bikes, or other unsupportive details.

As you consider the requirements you will use for determining who receives assistance, also consider your area's culture, climate and cost of living. As I mentioned earlier, poverty is not a simple dollar amount earned per day. Someone who lives in poverty lives in constant fear of crisis or starvation. They have no safety net if the weather turns bad or illness strikes. In the U.S., because we have no universal healthcare system, someone can live in poverty even though they own their own house and a car. If they have no savings and have to spend their wages on hospital bills, they will go hungry and perhaps lose their house and other property. In contrast, someone might live in a warm climate and have only a shack to sleep in. But if they own a small piece of land where they can grow food for themselves and to trade, they can have zero monetary income and still not be poor. If their culture, national policies and social support system of friends and family cover all potential crises, they will not live in poverty's fear of crisis.

One of the criteria that Grameen Bank uses in Bangladesh when determining an individual's qualification for assistance is the sturdiness of their house. Because Bangladesh suffers torrential rains during their rainy season, strong walls and a good roof mean the difference between dread of rain and confident comfort. With four strong walls, a sound roof and even a tiny income the individual will likely not qualify for assistance. You can find a list of their criteria on page 111 of *Creating a World Without Poverty*.

You and your team will have to designate your own criteria and requirements for qualifying individuals. Don't get lulled into common poverty measures like some arbitrary dollar amount earned per day. Look instead at quality of life criteria for your area and find your own line where people shift from contented comfort to constant fear and stress. Then develop criteria that will reveal individuals who truly need your program's assistance. A sliding scale might work best so that people who are living under the worst stress might qualify for nearly a full subsidy (remember to make them pay at least a small amount so they will value their bike, training or other services) while people who are only on the edge of poverty qualify for a micro loan instead. You can also combine the two. For instance someone might qualify for assistance in purchasing a

250 dollar bicycle. Because they have a low-paying job they can manage a loan, but not for the entire amount. In this case, a subsidy that pays for half of the bike could bring the price into the range where the new owner could pay the rest off with a micro loan. Look at all the combinations that make sense for your program and budget.

Now that we've covered the many ways you can serve the needs of disadvantaged people through your Social Bike Business program, it's time to move into setting up your career training program.

CHAPTER 8

Career Training & Program Refinement

Think of the career training part of your program as far more than just helping people find work. It gives you the stage you need to show your clients how much value lies inside of them. Simply by helping them achieve a defined set of new skills and knowledge, then rewarding them with certification as experts on that topic, you will help them discover a level of confidence they likely never imagined. On top of that, you can offer your star graduates the opportunity to give a hand to their neighbors by becoming trainers for your program.

One Street's recommended curriculum includes all of the pieces of a strong career training program. It captures the experiences of our local partners and advisors and ensures that the most important concepts in each career module are covered. But this chapter and the curriculum framework it covers do not include the specialties of you and your team. It also cannot include the unique needs of your culture, your community or the particular people you aim to serve with your program. That's why I will only outline the curriculum and offer suggested materials. It's up to you and your team to flesh out your own career training curriculum to fit the needs of your community. Consider partnering with other organizations and schools in your area that are already offering similar courses. Just beware of practices and curricula that veer away from your goals.

You will also need to carefully design your training program to ensure your most disadvantaged neighbors can attend. The best way to learn how to do this is to ask prospective students. Schedule classes during times convenient for them. If weekdays are usually work days, only schedule evening classes during the week. If weekends are critical for family activities, make it easy for them to bring their kids by offering childcare and plenty of breaks so your students can still spend time with their children. If your center isn't open yet, choose a location for your classes that's convenient to your priority students. Even if it is in or near their neighborhood, check first that it is a place they trust and respect.

Promoting your program will also require a deep understanding of the accepted communication methods for your community. Whether it's flyers, word-of-mouth, radio announcements, or door hangers, make your message clear including how much time will be required, how much it will cost if they don't qualify for a full scholarship, how they can apply for a scholarship, and where they can get more information. Use the language of your most disadvantaged neighbors, even in your simple advertisements so they will know they are welcome.

Each of your courses will cost your organization money, so price them at a rate that will cover all of these costs plus a bit more to ensure there is no loss. Scholarships—covered by donations, grants and other subsidy funding—are an important way to fill your classrooms with your target clients. Micro loans might also work for some. See the previous chapter for details on setting up your micro lending and subsidy programs as well as qualifying individuals. You can also have a waiting list for more advantaged students. If you don't fill the class with scholarship recipients, then invite these waitlist folks who will pay full price. While this will be a disappointment because your course won't be serving as many disadvantaged people as possible, at least you will gain practice and the tuition fees will help pay for the course costs. But don't forget that your bottom line is the number of disadvantaged people served, so do everything you can to fill those classroom seats with the people who need the training the most.

Determining the number of students per course is also important because with too many, the quality of training will drop. But with too few, you will have to charge too much or you won't cover the basic costs or serve as many people as you can. Find out what other career training programs charge in your area. Then study your detailed budget for your career training program to determine each course's full costs. Include trainer salaries, fees for expert speakers, room rental and utilities, training supplies, and what it costs your organization to administer the program. Then, just as with determining the price of the products you sell (more in the next chapter), choose a price that more than covers your costs at the ideal number of students per course.

Your career training program will be one of the highlights of your Social Bike Business program because it will give your clients the tools they need to leave poverty behind forever. But don't forget that everything you and your staff teach in your career training program will also help you refine your whole Social Bike Business program. In this

chapter you will read about our recommended career training modules:

1. Bike repair basics & teaching people to ride
2. Introduction to owning and operating a social bike shop
3. Merchandising & marketing
4. Business management
5. Sales & customer service
6. Advanced bike repair
7. Social bike manufacture

As you can see, every one of these modules not only applies to your program's clients who want to start a new career, but directly back to your program. So as you develop your own training courses, use the information you offer to gauge and adjust your own program and its services. Also note the ideas and revelations your students come up with during each course. As a teacher myself, I have often been astonished by what I learn from my students. Because most of the people who take your courses will be experts on the struggles of the next group of people you want to serve, their knowledge will be invaluable for refining your program.

Each module, as well as the full course, must be fleshed out with input from your leadership team and enlist local experts as trainers and speakers. Each module has its own certificate upon completion. These modules and their certificates are designed to assist participants in finding jobs both within and outside of the bicycle industry. For instance, business management can set them up to start any sort of business and customer service will give them everything they need to get a job at any retail or service business. Even the bicycle repair modules will teach them the basics of mechanical skills, which they can transfer to any mechanical or technical job.

Make sure to include the skills they will need to capture a job in each of the module topics. Emphasize being on time and dressing appropriately for interviews. A suit and tie or a dress might be helpful for a customer service position, but such clothing choices would be a detriment when interviewing for a mechanic's position. Also, in each of your module courses, include resume writing as a homework assignment. Look for the absolute basics: clean and free from errors, clear, maximum two pages, time sequence with as few gaps as possible, and inclusion of pertinent job and training experience that apply to the particular job only. Explain appropriate references to include (not family and friends). Role playing for interviews in class will also help build their confidence for what might be their first job interview. Your ongoing outreach to employers in your community might result in job openings during their training, which would be fortunate timing. Let all your trainees know that even if this doesn't work out, you will continue to help them find work.

Make full certification a reward for the successful completion of all six of the first six modules. Full certification should be required before your program will support a participant in the opening and operations of their own social bike shop. This will ensure that the social bike shop owners your program supports are fully committed to serving the needs of disadvantaged people and have been trained in the concepts necessary for success. Note that this full career training certification is different from the social bike shop certification that you should require annually to ensure that each shop is still focused on serving the needs of disadvantaged people and thus qualifies for your program's continued assistance. The full career training certification is a one time certification for the prospective social bike shop owner; something they can display as their own accomplishment. I'll discuss your support of social bike shops in Chapter 10.

Another very important role for the graduates of these modules is as trainers for your career training program. Your early courses will likely be taught by you, the other founders of your organization and local experts on each topic. This is okay, because you have to start somewhere. But as soon as you graduate your first class, find the stars who are ready to give back to your program. Ask them if they'd like to teach and offer them a market wage as an expert trainer. By hiring trainers who your target students know and respect, their neighbors, you will lift your career training program to a whole new level. It will shift from advantaged people teaching disadvantaged people to peers learning from each other.

Social bike manufacture, the seventh module, stands on its own and should mainly be offered to people you hope to hire to manufacture your program's bikes. By hiring them, you will also give them the on-the-job experience that is needed for such a specialty craft. The star graduates from this module will also become its best trainers. You'll read more about manufacturing in Chapter 11.

The hours marked below in the descriptions for each module are our estimate for the minimum classroom time needed to cover the material. These hours do not include homework and projects outside of class time. In general, I recommend that you expect your students to spend the same amount of hours outside of class exploring and trying out the material they learn. So, a module with 20 hours marked, will actually be at least 40 hours of effort for each student.

The learning outcomes listed for each module should give you an idea of how to gauge your students' accomplishments in the course. They will help you gauge the progress of each of your students. If a student doesn't meet your expected learning outcomes, do not certify them! Let all your students know at the start exactly what your expectations are for them in order to pass and be certified. Deliver this info in writing and several times verbally during the first few class sessions to give them a chance to ask questions. This will help ease the disappointment of any students who don't achieve the minimum needed to be certified because they will be familiar with the expected learning outcomes. By sticking to your requirements, you will keep your certifications at a high standard so they will hold weight when graduates show them to prospective employers.

1) Bike repair basics & teaching people to ride (20 hours):
This module includes some classroom time, but also must include hands-on repairs for each student to complete. It also includes working with new riders to practice teaching safe riding skills.

The best manual I have found for teaching bicycle repair is *Bicycle Maintenance & Repair*, by Todd Downs. It is the only one that still includes some basic parts and older bikes. Even so, it is quite heavy on very fancy sport bikes. This is okay especially since these bikes are covered in more detail in the advanced bike repair module. So I recommend using this same book for both modules. Students interested in getting a job at a for-profit bike shop will need to take both modules.

The bicycle repair section of this course will require approximately 16 of its 20 hours of classroom time. Hire experienced bicycle mechanics as trainers.

Start by discussing: types of bikes, proper bike fit, naming parts of a bike, basic diagnosis of problems including checking for proper air pressure, worn tires, damaged rims, brake effectiveness, loose bearings, bent or broken frame and fork, and any loose or suspicious parts. Also show them how to determine the function of a part and use slow elimination for diagnosis. Spend quality time teaching students proper use of tools and reinforce this throughout the course. Have them practice diagnosis and test each student one-on-one with three bikes you've set up with different problems. Ask students who do not pass this test to work extra hours with the trainers until they can pass.

Next, show them and have them practice basic, important repairs including: installing tires and tubes, airing tires, (rim repair and wheel truing are in the advanced module), repairing and adjusting brakes, adjusting all four bearing units (two hubs, headset and bottom bracket), checking and tightening all other parts with proper torque (wheels, pedals,

handlebars, stems, cranks and small parts).

In the final section on repair, show them and have them practice: removing and installing a chain including proper chain length, best cleaners to use, use of the proper type of lube, adjusting gears, and what to look for during a test ride after a repair job is finished. Spend time explaining the three levels of viscosities of lubes used on bikes—very light oil, regular oil, bicycle-grade grease—and their proper use.

The section on teaching people to ride is also a critical part of this module because anyone who takes a job at your center, at a for-profit bike shop or opens their own shop must have the skills to convey this information to their customers. Unsafe riding habits are the cause of far too many bicycle crashes. Students who graduate from this module will become the sort of mentors who can change such dangerous behavior. Teach this part of the module with an emphasis on how the students would teach others these skills. Simply teaching your students these safe riding skills will not help them overcome the awkwardness of guiding someone out of a habit they are accustomed to. Check with your local bicycle advocacy organization to see if they have any ready-made safe riding materials you can use as handouts. Practice all of the skills with your students, first on quiet streets and finally in traffic. Then have your students teach these skills to new riders and discuss their stories, concerns and successes in class.

Include in this safe riding section: bicycle safety check (same as above, but vital for ensuring the person can ride safely), proper fit for a bike including bike size and seat post height, ride with traffic (never against traffic), obey all traffic laws, ride predictably, signal turns, take the travel lane if there is not enough room for cars to pass and speeds are low, don't ride on sidewalks, find the safest routes and avoid high speed roads with no room for bikes, and always use lights at night. Additionally, discuss creative and safe ways of carrying loads and children because these are often barriers that keep disadvantaged people from choosing bicycling.

One warning I must add here is to avoid pushing bicycle helmets. Bicycle helmets are only designed to offer minor protection in crashes up to 12 miles per hour. They offer little protection in a major car/bike crash and they never prevent crashes. Understanding their limits is important. But far more important is that bicycle helmet promotions undermine any effort to increase bicycling, including Social Bike Business programs. Bicyclists suffer *fewer* head injuries than pedestrians and car occupants. Yet only bicyclists are singled out to wear helmets. I won't get into the bizarre reasons for this here. If you're interested, you can read more on our Bicycle Helmets page under the Resources section of the One Street website. Avoid shock horror helmet promotions that set bicycling out as far more dangerous than it actually is. Such scare tactics only scare people away from bicycling.

Learning outcomes:
- Repair – basic understanding of bicycle types and bicycle fit, proper diagnosis, proper use of tools, successful repairs for all types covered.
- Teaching riding – a respectful, caring ability to teach others all the safe riding skills covered.

2) Introduction to owning and operating a social bike shop (16 hours): As you will read in Chapter 10, the social bike shops that you support through your program must also serve the needs of disadvantaged people. Their bottom line must be the number of disadvantaged people they serve, just as with your program. In fact, these shops will be an extension of your program. So all the lessons you and your team have learned in launching your program will be great material for this module.

Start the course by discussing: how your program can support their social bike shop (details in Chapter 10), annual certification requirements, the difference between a social bike shop and a for-profit bike shop and deciding which is best for them (students who would prefer to own a for-profit business can skip this module), and overcoming common misconceptions about serving the bicycling needs of disadvantaged people. Also include discussions on how best to welcome the most disadvantaged people. This could include role playing.

Round out the rest of the course with: choosing a location in a distressed neighborhood not already served by a bike shop that invites disadvantaged people (field trips would work well here), clean look for their shop and professional signage, hours that serve the needs of disadvantaged residents of the neighborhood, elements of transportation bikes, learning from their customers to improve their shop offerings, an overview of all of the other modules (except bicycle manufacture), and how they could expand what they learned for launching other types of social businesses that serve disadvantaged people.

If you can invite an owner of a local for-profit bike shop to speak at a few of your classes, this could help to underscore the difficulty of succeeding in this business. Such an owner could offer mistakes and solutions they've discovered over their years in business. Make sure they focus on their business as a whole and don't spend too much time on product details because as a for-profit shop they have to focus only on expensive, fancy sport bikes that don't apply to social bike shops. For information on preventing common bike shop struggles, find an example of a bike shop employee manual on the Bike Shops page under Resources on the One Street website.

Learning outcomes:
- Clear understanding of the difference between a social bike shop

and a for-profit bike shop,
- Ability to articulate the bike shop and bicycle needs of disadvantaged people,
- Ability to identify appropriate locations for social bike shops, and
- Basic understanding of the information offered in the other modules.

3) Merchandising & marketing (16 hours): Merchandising and marketing may seem like separate topics, but they are in fact inseparable. A business owner could do a brilliant marketing campaign, but if all those new customers came in to find strange products and scattered, confusing displays, the marketing campaign would fail.

Start this course by discussing: branding and name protection, best practices in merchandising and marketing, balancing costs, avoiding paid advertisement, how to get free advertisement through news stories and partner organizations, why word-of-mouth is the best way to market (requires great service and the right products), how your bicycle community center can help, using a website and always directing news stories and social media back to that site.

In the last part of the course, dig into hands-on projects including: comparing good and bad merchandising displays, group projects to create displays (perhaps even a contest), field trips to good and bad retail examples (including bike shops as well as other types of stores) followed by thorough discussions on what worked and what didn't, and homework assignments for students to notice what sort of marketing works on them and people they know.

If you know an owner of a retail store that is not a bike shop who could speak to your class, they could offer insight into merchandising and marketing from a new angle.

Learning outcomes:
- Understanding of effective merchandising,
- Ability to create excellent product displays, and
- Ability to create a strong marketing plan that fits a tight budget.

4) Business management (20 hours): In the next chapter, I'll go into detail on the vital elements of good business management in the context of running your Social Bike Business program at your bicycle community center. All of these will apply to this module, too. Be sure to discuss: planning and budgeting, thorough bookkeeping to discover *all* costs and assess the true profit margin, insurance, warranties, collecting sales tax, legal requirements, hiring and managing staff, pricing and inventory control, and how the other module topics fit into good management (repair service, merchandising & marketing, and sales & customer service). Make sure that your curriculum for this course covers

each element well, especially for aspiring social bike shop owners, but also folks interested in owning or managing other types of businesses.

Field trips and student projects can include discussions with business owners as well as employees. Homework should include balancing checkbooks, studying profit and loss statements, and creating their own profit and loss statement (P&L) for an imaginary business. Role playing of disgruntled employee situations and angry customer encounters would also be useful.

Potential speakers could include an accountant, a business owner, and a small business consultant perhaps from your local chamber of commerce or college.

Learning outcomes:
- Ability to plan and budget within reason to include profits,
- Understanding of the legal requirements of running a small business in your community,
- Demonstration of skills to work through difficult employee and customer situations, and
- Understanding of the key concepts of pricing and inventory control.

5) Sales & customer service (16 hours): This module should first cover pricing, inventory control, running a professional bicycle repair service department, and merchandising to ensure students understand the framework needed to serve their customers. But the most important focus will be on how to do an excellent job of serving the needs of their customers. We have all been poorly programmed by bad sales representatives who ask if we need help then do their best to hide from us. The only way small businesses can compete with the big box retailers is to offer extraordinary customer service.

Start by discussing the elements of great customer service including: greeting customers, engaging them in conversation that reveals what they are looking for, avoiding yes or no questions (that means never asking, "Do you need help?"), building trust, helping them find what they need (offer no more than the two or three best choices), and offering more products and services they may have forgotten. Discuss why product features must only be offered in relation to what the customer needs and why the conversation must be about the customer, not the sales person. Then drive home the need to close the sale—they've got to ask the customer if they'd like to buy the product now. Note that these concepts also apply to answering their business's phone.

Consider field trips to retailers during class, though homework assignments to field test these concepts might work better because the students would be less conspicuous entering retail stores alone. Have them report in class about their experiences. You can also have students try to sell each other products and then discuss as a class what they did well and what needed work. One important challenge to practice is to prevent the customer from saying, "No, just looking." Then, if the customer actually proclaims this dead-end statement, have your students try different methods of restarting the conversation. Also have them test sales people during their field trips to see if any manage to get them talking again after they've said, "No, just looking."

If you can find a great salesperson or a sales consultant to speak to your class, this could be helpful. There are also countless books and manuals available on good sales and customer service practices. Check your library for books that will give you more ideas for teaching these concepts. Find some examples of how to hold employees to good sales and customer service practices in the example of a bike shop employee manual on the Bike Shops page under Resources on the One Street website.

Learning outcomes:
- An in depth understanding of pricing and inventory control,
- Demonstration of basic merchandising concepts,
- Proper set up of a bicycle repair service area, and
- Demonstration of sales skills with even the most difficult customers.

6) Advanced bike repair (20 hours, prerequisite: module #1 or similar experience): This module builds on the bike repair concepts covered in the basic bike repair module. Students must master difficult repairs before receiving certification so include lots of hands-on practice time. It also includes in depth study of and practice working with the latest high-end sport racing bikes. Even though social bike shops do not carry such bikes, these skills are required for full certification of students interested in opening their own social bike shop because, as a full-service bike shop they will encounter sport bikes brought in by customers. Students who are interested in working at a for-profit bike shop will also need to take this module because such shops specialize in these bikes.

You will need to employ a master bicycle mechanic as a trainer for the entire course. This mechanic must have experience with the latest sport bikes. Make sure that he or she spends lots of time on review and hands-on practice of the material covered. Our recommended book for the course is the same used in the basic module: *Bicycle Maintenance & Repair*, by Todd Downs.

Start by reviewing the main topics covered in the basic course as a refresher as well as to ensure students who qualified through experience rather than taking the basic module have reviewed these topics.

Be sure to include: full bicycle overhaul (find an overhaul checklist in the Appendix section), advanced diagnosis, identifying cracks and unacceptable wear, replacing worn parts, particulars about social bikes that serve your community's needs, mismatched parts, chain alignment, use of specialized tools, mechanical theories, torque and other measurements, wheel truing and building, suspension service, disk brakes, overhauling coaster brakes and internal gear hubs, working with carbon fiber and titanium, servicing other specialty parts and finding manufacturer specs.

Learning outcomes:
- Advanced diagnosis and
- Mastery of all repairs covered in this course.

7) Social bike manufacturing (demonstration of skills, rather than hours): This module is separate from the first six modules since it is not required for certification as a social bike shop owner, but will be required for your welders and assemblers once your bike manufacturing is underway. Welding training will include a gradual increase in difficulty from practice metal to bicycle racks to welding of frames. Early welding training can take place at a partner institution such as a community college or vocational school. But they must learn TIG welding of steel. Any other type of welding or metal is not suitable for the manufacture of social bikes.

Students need to progress from welding flat steel to pipe steel. Practice metal can progress from scrap to the tubular steel you use for your bike racks and finally to frame and fork steel. Each student should be required to complete the manufacture of one whole bicycle for their own use before you certify them. Include the cost of steel, paint and parts of these bikes in your fee for this module.

Students in this module can weld the bike racks for your program, whether to be added to your bikes or sold separately, as long as the racks pass inspection. But only the graduates who you hire as employees should be allowed to weld bike frames and forks to be assembled and sold at your center.

Classroom time should be minimal because hands-on skill development is primary. In classroom sessions, students will learn about bicycle design concepts for disadvantaged people, metal fabrication and strengths (focused on steel), quality testing, painting and assembly. Since this module will focus on hands-on training, find more details in Chapter 11.

Learning outcomes:
- Mastery of welding bicycle frames, forks and racks; and
- Mastery of painting and assembling new bikes.

Now that you've seen what you'll need to launch your career training program, let's look at best practices for managing your bicycle community center. Even if you have to launch your career training program before your center is open, you can now imagine how your graduates can help you at your center. Opening your center as soon as possible will ensure you can tap their expertise to the fullest.

CHAPTER 9

Managing Your Center

Your bicycle community center will become the heart of your Social Bike Business program, a beacon to people who have otherwise been abandoned by society. Just as it is vital to establish your organization with particular elements for it to grow strong, you will need to set in place important systems at your center to ensure you can help every disadvantaged person who enters, find what they need. Because your center can also become the mother ship for social bike shops owned by graduates of your career training program, it must be an excellent model for business management.

Business management resembles the oversight that nonprofit leaders give to their organization, but in a microcosm. Rather than envisioning impact on the entire community as an organization must, a business manager fixates on the location, primping and priming it for each customer who enters. Even marketing and advertising is entirely focused on encouraging people to come to that location. Leaders of Social Bike Business programs must wear both hats—organization leader and business manager. This is actually a good thing because the two roles are complimentary, that is, as long as you don't get the two roles mixed up. For instance, it would be quite easy for an organization leader to spend their time in partner meetings discussing what the program can offer to particular groups of people, but forget that once those people arrive, the bicycle community center must be a well oiled machine that's ready to deliver. On the other extreme, a leader who is more comfortable preparing a location could have everything in order and ready to serve, but without the partner outreach and trust of the community, no one will show up. A Social Bike Business is not an ordinary business, so you can't expect people to understand it as soon as the sign goes up.

This dual role requirement can, and should sound daunting. That's why I recommend hiring a manager for your center as soon as possible. You would look for the sort of person who loves details and wants to make your center thrive. This will leave you and the rest of your leadership team in the broader vision realm where you're most needed.

Hiring a manager is just one example of why staffing is a top concern of business management at your center. In this chapter I will overview this and other key systems you will need in place. Look for these sections:

- Budgeting and Assessing Profit and Loss Statements
- Hiring and Training Your Center's Manager and Staff Team
- Staff vs. Board Roles
- Purchasing, Pricing and Inventory Turns
- Merchandising and Displays
- Customer Service and Sales
- Branding, Marketing and Promotion
- Bookkeeping, Collecting Sales Tax and Reporting
- Insurance, Warranties and Other Legal Requirements

Budgeting and Assessing Profit & Loss Statements

As I discussed earlier, your organization will have a full annual budget that covers all your programs and administration expenses. This overarching budget might have just a few line items that capture the total expenses you expect for your center. But in order to do a great job of managing your center and all of its intricate, moving parts, you will need a separate budget just for your center that breaks these totals into detail. The most useful format for such a business-oriented budget is a cash flow chart. Just like your organization's annual budget, this cash flow chart will include line items for income and expenses. It will also include your estimates per month for each. You can set this up in a spreadsheet like Excel and include formulas in the cells that calculate the resulting cash on hand each month; that is, funding available in your bank account. At the end of each month, you can change your budgeted amounts to the actual amounts that occurred and make adjustments into the future.

Such a cash flow budgeting system will show you when money will be tight and when money can be spent. You will know whether a big order for parts is possible or whether waiting a month or two would be wiser. Find a sample cash flow chart, complete with formulas, on the One Street website under Management in the left menu. This sample is for a full organization but should be easy to adapt for a detailed center cash flow chart. Add income lines for sales, service, and career training fees and remove fundraising income unless your center will have its own fundraising mechanisms. Also, in addition to your projected wages you plan to pay your employees, add other employee expense line items. In the U.S., these amount to about thirty percent of the total wages. These employee expenses will include taxes, workers compensation insurance and/or other payments for employees required by your particular government.

To allow for unexpected expenses, slightly round up each of your projected expense totals and even add some expenses toward the end of the year that would be helpful, but not necessary. This will help you and your team strive for your ideal income and be prepared for any set backs that may occur. After you've used this cash flow system to manage your center's expenditures you might like to create one for your entire organization, which could then include your projected fundraising income straight from your annual budget.

In this cash flow budget for your center, be sure to separate your equipment costs (these are one time costs); fixed costs that recur such as salaries, supplies, phone and utilities; and your inventory costs. Later in this chapter I will go into more detail on bookkeeping and recommended categories for recording actual income and expenses. For now, you simply need to understand the difference between these three types of expenditures. By separating them, you will start to see patterns such as recurring costs each month and certain times of year that require more expenditure for replenishing inventory or investing in new equipment. These patterns and expectations will help you avoid spending money you will need in an upcoming month.

When you first open your center and create your cash flow budget, start as small as you possibly can. For instance, if demand for bicycle repair is small, consider only equipping one repair station until you can raise the funds to equip more. When ordering your first parts and accessories to sell, learn the absolute necessities you will have to stock and avoid items that your customers won't necessarily need. Later, when income is rolling in, you can fill out your inventory with less vital, fun items that inspire impulse purchases from your customers.

In the bookkeeping section later in this chapter I will overview methods of recording your daily receipts into your ledger on your computer with a bookkeeping program, likely QuickBooks. This bookkeeping ledger will convert your daily income and expense figures into what is known as your profit and loss (P&L) statements. You can create monthly, year-to-date and annual P&L statements that will show you an accurate picture of income generation and costs that were required to generate that income. Every successful business owner is skilled at assessing their P&L statements because they are exact snapshots of the performance of the business. Needed changes become hard to ignore. For instance, a bike shop that employs four full-time sales people but only sold one bike in a month will either need to invest a lot of time in changing staff and providing sales training or, if the market isn't there, perhaps cutting back on sales staff. Without an honest assessment of the P&L

statement, the owner or manager could easily continue on the same path toward business failure.

Another invaluable benefit of P&L statements is that they will clearly show you and your team the full cost of running your center. Novice business owners often make the mistake of only calculating the cost of the products they sell and then expecting any markup they make to be full profit to them. They forget about all the other expenses they have just to switch the lights on in their store. Such shortsightedness could be disastrous to your Social Bike Business program and your bicycle community center.

Most retail businesses use a markup of fifty percent (also called "keystone") as their target. This means that they will sell a product that costs them ten dollars from their wholesaler for twenty dollars. All you mathematicians out there will argue that this is actually a one hundred percent markup. This is true, but in retail, a one hundred percent markup is referred to as a fifty percent markup because the markup is fifty percent of the retail price.

People who have not owned a business for any significant amount of time will think that this is a massive profit, that all retailers are rolling in cash. You will think this. Your board members will think this. Your staff will think this. And all of your customers will think this. The only people in this misguided group that absolutely must change their perspective are you, your board members and your key staff. For all others, it's best to simply hide your wholesale prices because none of the others will pay attention long enough for you to explain all the costs of running a business. In fact, the most successful retailers, retailers who mark some items up well above keystone, are lucky if they make one percent profit! As hard as it may be to believe, you and your team will have to fight and scratch to achieve this elusive one percent profit from your center even after marking up all of your products to keystone or above.

This is why I can't emphasize enough how harmful discounting is to your program. By understanding this ultimate goal of a meager one percent profit you will see that giving just a ten dollar discount will require your staff to sell another one thousand dollars of products just to make up for it. Even if you have a fun and flexible personality, in order to run a profitable center, you will have to morph into a hardnosed, rigid dictator whenever any of your staff want to offer customers a discount.

In order to reach this elusive one percent profit, you and your team will have to assess your center's P&L statements with careful scrutiny or employ a manager that has this skill. What you discover in these P&L statements will help you refine your budgeting process for better accuracy. As I mentioned earlier, you'll want to adjust your full organization's budget with your board of directors at least once halfway through the year. Tune your center's cash flow budget in alignment with these adjustments in order to be prepared for upcoming expenses and to have realistic expectations for income.

While fundraising will be an important part of your whole organization's projected income, keep it out of your center's cash flow budgeting process. You need your center to be self-sufficient, not a drain on the organization. You also want to avoid financial threats to your center when fundraising efforts fall short. Even the fundraising you do to cover subsidies for your most disadvantaged customers needs to be recorded separately from your center's bookkeeping and instead recorded in your organization's administrative bookkeeping. Thus, the number of subsidies you offer will be fully dependent on the funds raised. From your center's management viewpoint, the subsidies are simply the means of payment for these particular customers and need to be recorded just like any other sale. This will ensure that the daily costs of the center are covered by the products and services it manages to sell.

Hiring and Training Your Center's Manager and Staff Team

Before you broadcast your job announcements, you'll need to make sure you're ready for employees. Check with your government for all the requirements. In the U.S., once your organization has incorporated and achieved 501(c)(3) status you will have your federal employer identification number (EIN), which you will use on all your employment paperwork.

In order for your center to do a great job of serving the bicycle needs of the most disadvantaged people through topnotch management as well as offering jobs, you will need to designate two categories of employees: 1) managers, 2) regular staff.

As you can imagine after reading this far, managing your center will require special skills and previous experience. This means that your first manager will likely not be disadvantaged. In the future, once your career training is underway and you've filled several regular staff positions from the neighborhood you can look for stars to promote to the management level.

For this first management position, if you do find someone with management skills who is currently struggling and a resident of a distressed neighborhood, this would be a bonus. More likely, you will have to spread your manager job announcement far and wide to find someone who not only has these skills, but is passionate about your organization's mission. You might not have the means to pay the full market rate for managers in your area, especially if you're in a wealthy city, but many talented leaders would prefer to take a meaningful job like yours rather than a high paying job at a company that is destructive to society. Be sure to start with and highlight this social benefit of the job in your job announcement. Use every networking channel you and your helpers have available. Seek out similar organizations who can help you spread the word. Use your website, your e-newsletter and all your social media channels because people who are already connected to you and your organization are your most likely candidates. You can even approach talented people you've noticed working in other fields who might not have considered applying for your job. Include in the job announcement specific directions such as:

- Send a cover letter, resume and three work-related references
- The exact method of delivery such as through the mail or email
- The deadline for receipt of applications

Discard any applications that arrive without these specifics or after the deadline because this will demonstrate an inability to follow rules and directions. You need a team player, not a self-serving rogue.

Then begin reading the remaining applications with an open mind. I've learned over my three decades of hiring and managing staff that the cover letter is far more important than the resume because a resume can be copied and sent to many potential employers. Only the cover letter can be crafted for you alone. If it starts with a general salutation and uses general terms for any job, you know the applicant couldn't care less about your organization or managing your center. Discard the application. If the cover letter does use your name and mentions your organization, but says nothing about helping people with bicycles, discard the application. Beyond these obvious revelations, a cover letter can also reveal your top candidates through phrases of passion or particular abilities you're looking for in your manager. Over the years, I've learned to hardly look at the resumes included in applicant's packets. When I do, I ignore academic achievements because being sequestered away in a safe institution does very little to prepare people for the realities of life. Job experience, unusual achievements and volunteer activities offer far more insight into a candidate's talents and abilities.

Once you've narrowed the applicants to those worthy of an interview, ask questions pertinent to the position and avoid time wasters like clever riddles or questions about their happiest moment as a child. Knowing the pertinent questions requires you and your fellow leaders to first fully assess the position and the skills needed to thrive in it. If you are interviewing for the general manager of your center, ask them questions that will reveal their ability to juggle many tasks and remain supportive to staff and clients even as they resolve a crisis behind the scenes. Also find a way for them to reveal their level of passion for helping disadvantaged people. The most talented manager from a top corporation who has no such passion would be a terrible hire for your center.

If you want to explore some fascinating new trends in hiring great talent, I highly recommend reading *The Rare Find: Spotting Exceptional Talent Before Everyone Else*, by George Anders. He talks about ingenious methods used to find the best candidates for important jobs, many of which do not include resumes. Those that do, use a method he calls reading resumes upside down, in other words, skimming over academic and employment achievements to find the spark of genius such as a wildly successful lemonade stand in childhood or saving the life of a friend on a backpacking trip.

Look for attributes that demonstrate leadership ability; not dictatorship, but the sort of leader people will be proud to follow. Find out if an applicant has persisted when faced with a series of barriers or rebounded after a devastating disappointment. Find out if they spend time analyzing their failures because these are the sorts of people who will grow into great leaders. On the negative side, avoid complainers or applicants who blame others or external forces for things that went wrong. Only good leaders are comfortable taking responsibility for their actions.

This person will become the leader of the other staff at your center. Staff members will only answer to the manager, not board members, so you and the rest of the leadership team will have to trust this person to care for and nurture the other employees even as he or she ensures each staff member is doing their job. At the start, you will likely only have room for one manager, but as your program grows, you might find that adding specific manager positions will increase your program's effectiveness. For instance, you could add a career training program manager or a bicycle manufacture program manager.

Once your program is running at full steam, your managers can train and groom your regular staff members who show management talent to eventually move into this higher lever position. Either way, you've got to have a very formal and arduous hiring process for any manager level position to ensure your center can do a great job serving people who need its services.

On the other hand, your regular staff should be made up of disadvantaged people who are simply eager for a job, even from the very beginning. As your career training program kicks in, you can encourage graduates to apply for open positions. I've also heard of social businesses with the extreme hiring policy of giving any open job to the first disadvantaged person to apply. This avoids the resume and interview process that could scare off potential stars who have never been trained in job search practices.

Note that even with this first-to-apply approach you will still need to have each new employee fill out an application with all their contact info and any forms required by your government. In the U.S., these include forms W-4 and I-9, both of which you can find on the web at www.irs.gov. States in the U.S. often have their own required forms in addition to these federal forms. Check with the pertinent agencies in your government. Create a separate file for each employee you hire and keep these records for the life of your organization.

The payroll process adds enormously to your bookkeeping tasks.

While experienced managers will have no problem handling this time-intensive job, I still recommend hiring an outside accountant to take care of it. This will free up your manager for tasks at your center. Also, if you hire the same accountant to do your payroll as well as your annual tax paperwork, all the payroll info will already be in their computer, streamlining the process.

I recommend keeping your regular staff members on an hourly wage, especially as they learn the concepts of good work habits, but consider giving your managers an annual salary, at least after they've proven their leadership abilities. A steady paycheck will give them more confidence in their financial situations and help them focus on pursuing your center's goals.

With a first-to-apply hiring policy in place for your regular employees (never your managers or executive director), you would have to match it with a strict break-in period, perhaps three or six months when they are paid minimum wage and very little is invested in them (no uniform, no business cards, etc.). During this time period they will need to learn and stick to the rules of your center, demonstrate the principles of serving their most disadvantaged neighbors, do their job well, and become a valued part of your center's team before you advance them into a full staff position. I recommend having a high tolerance for slip ups, because good work habits take time to learn and many of the people you hire this way will have never had the opportunity to learn these skills. But you or your manager will have to have a clear concept of when bad behaviors are doing more harm than is tolerable.

If you or your manager has to fire someone during or even after this break-in period, your goal must be for the person to appreciate it. I know that sounds strange, but it is vital. Your organization was not founded to devastate people, not even those with the worst behavior problems. Being hired may have been one of their proudest moments. To be fired could throw them into unimaginable depths. If you are not the one to have to do this unfortunate task, train and retrain your managers to make every firing as respectful, compassionate and educational as it can possibly be.

As a bike shop owner I had to go through this gut wrenching ritual far too many times. Drinking on the job, bad mouthing the shop to customers, and stealing were some of the behaviors that tipped the scale for me. But even with employees who had committed such harm, I always did my best to make them feel good about being fired. If the offense was not extreme, I gave them a clear warning first. I recommend putting such a warning in writing. But if the offense was extreme or a repeat after my warning, I'd let them know the situation was serious, take them to a private room and begin by asking them what they expected to happen when they did what they did. In the very best cases, I let them do ninety percent of the talking and by the time we both stood up, they had basically fired themselves quite happily. Employees who do harm to your organization often do so because they are no longer interested in the job, but don't have the courage to quit. Being fired, if it is done respectfully, can come as a great relief to them.

Even with the most stringent hiring processes only half of your workers will choose to stick around for more than six months anyway. Maybe the job isn't right for them or they find another opportunity. By combining this clear break-in period with hiring the first to apply, you will actually increase the competition for your jobs and the determination of your workers to surpass that break-in period.

Consider having a break-in period for managers as well. You can call it a training period when this manager-in-training learns your organization's systems and principles and gets to know all its leaders. This will allow time for a bad hire to be revealed while avoiding the full pay and costs of supporting a full manager.

Detailed guidelines are the key to great job performance. Starting with your job descriptions and leading into your center's employee handbook, every required task and policy employees need to follow must be spelled out clearly. You can be more general and vague with a manager's job description because such a leadership role must have room for adapting to countless opportunities and crises. However, for your staff positions, the more detail the better. For instance, one task might be to keep the welcome area clean, but it must be spelled out to include details such as: Daily—dust furniture, bikes and displays; replace books in bookshelves; empty trash cans and sort out recyclables; dust mop floor; clean glass; Weekly—wet mop floor. By detailing expectations, including principles and policies, you or your manager can point to these expectations and respectfully ask employees to change bad behaviors. Show them where they missed then point to the guidelines as the proper method. Without clear guidelines, such requests could offend well-meaning employees. Find examples of detailed employee handbooks on One Street's website under Management in the left menu. The bike shop sample will be most pertinent to your center's employees.

You and your managers cannot leave your employee handbook on paper. In order for all those tasks, principles and policies to come alive for your employees you've got to engage an ongoing training system. As manager and director at nonprofits and owner of my bike shop, I learned after much trial and error that constant training and constant feedback are the only way to go. Of course, you must start with a concise training program for every employee's first week. This includes going over all the priorities in your handbook and having the new hire practice them so that you can offer praise and ideas for improvement. But do not let the training end after that first week. And never fall for the outmoded concept of annual reviews that only give managers an excuse to avoid reprimanding an employee for poor performance. Instead, train yourself and your managers to constantly offer employees constructive ways to improve and change bad behavior into effective work. When offering this feedback, start with a kind compliment and end with words of encouragement. Imagine a nutritious sandwich made with delicious bread that surrounds the necessary filling that would be sour delivered alone.

A concept that compliments hiring the first to apply is launching employees out of your program. Because your bottom line is the number of disadvantaged people served, you will never be able to pay the highest salaries for the level of expertise many of your employees will reach. For instance, your top customer service employee could easily move into a top sales job if he or she wanted to and your most talented welders could move from your highest paying welding position (likely under ten dollars an hour) into a master welder position at a metal fabricating company that could triple or quadruple their pay. In order to meet your bottom line, you and your manager will have to look for signs of talent and encourage these stars to move on. I recommend spending quality time networking with nearby employers in similar fields so that when you discover top talent through your program, you can help these stars negotiate for their dream job. Not only will you be helping these talented folks reach their potential, you will keep the cycle moving as your next stars step up to discover their untapped talents and then move on.

The Rare Find ends with a profound wake up call to those of us tasked with hiring people. The author notes the untold wasted talent that slips by institutionalized hiring procedures because of weak resumes or poor academic performance. He then lays the responsibility on us to capture these talented stars through better hiring procedures that focus on finding talent because "the benefits to society are likely to be much greater than the personal gain." This is at the end of a book written for leaders of for-profit corporations. Your center, with its social mission will be in a better position than any top corporation for seeking out and finding talented people who otherwise may never have been discovered. By helping discouraged people launch their careers, you will break them out of self-defeating cycles and show them how to offer their talents to the world.

Volunteers and Contractors

A few more roles you will want to differentiate include volunteers and contractors. Neither of these roles can be considered employees.

If you pay a volunteer with anything, whether cash or product, you will run the risk of being fined by your government for not recording this person as a paid employee. Be very clear with your volunteers that they are not employees. Only give them jobs that are not critical to your program's operation. Before inviting volunteers to help out, set up a strong system that includes job tasks spelled out, staff designated as volunteer supervisors, a means to record their hours served, and regular ways of thanking them for their service. Food is a biggy. Whenever volunteers put in more than a few hours, be sure to give them healthy snacks and drinks. I've also heard good things about earn-a-bike programs where volunteers can donate a set amount of hours to earn the chance to pick out a bike that has not been designated for refurbishing and build it up for themselves. If you add an earn-a-bike program, stipulate that the volunteer must pay for any parts needed to complete the bike and ensure that the earn-a-bike program is never confused with your program to provide safe, fully refurbished bikes to people in need. You don't want disadvantaged people getting the impression that they have to volunteer time they simply do not have in order to get a bike which they have to build themselves.

Contractors are also not employees of your organization. These are specialists such as your accountant, your plumber and your website designer. Working with contractors can be enticing because they are entirely responsible for handling all their own bookkeeping. All you have to do is pay them. Because of this, many young nonprofit organizations make the mistake of hiring their executive director, manager and other staff as contractors. In the U.S., this is *illegal*! A contractor is a sole proprietor, in business for themselves. They must be open for many other clients besides your organization. Unfortunately, there's enough grey area that these organizations usually get away with it.

Even beyond the legality issue, hiring a director or manager on contract sends them the signal that they are not actually part of the organization—not good for developing someone into a dedicated leader. Even a lower staff position will get this signal. Plus, if you hire them as a contractor rather than an employee, they can't claim the job as employment history on their resume except as a special note under their sole proprietorship as a contractor. So, never hire *any* of your staff, managers or otherwise, as contractors. Keep this designation for outside experts you hire for occasional, short term specialty jobs. And note that if any of these contractors do not have their own registered business, you will have to report what you paid them to your government. In the U.S., if you pay a non-employee who does not own a registered business more than six hundred dollars, you will need to submit form 1099 to the IRS and send a copy to the contractor.

Staff vs. Board Roles

In Chapter 2 I discussed the different leadership roles of board members and the executive director. By now, I hope you have decided to take one or the other role because anyone who reads this far in this book is sure to be leadership material. The most obvious difference between these two roles is that board members are not paid and executive directors are paid. This makes the executive director the top staff position.

The more important difference between these two roles is that board members keep their sights on the broad vision and their duties focused on the overall governance of the organization. In contrast, and quite complimentary, the executive director spends his or her day in the midst of all the action. This leader will personally know all staff, all key partners and all the important officials the organization is working with. They are responsible for the day-to-day details that ensure the success of the organization including all instructions and communications with the other staff. Board members must leave these daily duties to the executive director to avoid confusion and chaos.

Now that we have moved into management concepts of your center, another layer of your organization's chart has emerged—your managers. At the start of your Social Bike Business program, the executive director could fill the role of center manager, but this set up won't last long if your program is successful. The executive director needs to oversee all daily tasks, including the administration, fundraising and outreach necessary to the success of the entire organization. A thriving bicycle community center will need at least one manager to ensure that every person who comes in is served well.

The most common and proven organization structure ensures that managers only answer to the executive director, never board members. Staff at your center will work with and answer to their manager who then only reports important achievements and extreme concerns to the executive director. This leaves the daily decisions at the center to the manager, which frees up the executive director's time to take care of the organization as a whole.

There are other organization structures that place everyone at equal levels. These are less common and prone to redundancy, confusion and chaos caused by staff not knowing whom to seek for guidance. Communication and clarity become difficult without defined roles. Before setting up a less conventional organization structure, study successful models carefully. Remember that most people are not leaders. Your staff will want to come to work and know exactly who can tell them what they need to do that day. Whichever structure you choose, make sure this basic function is in place.

Purchasing, Pricing and Inventory Turns

The most enticing hazard for any leader of a retail business is purchasing. Once you have successfully applied for and received credit accounts at various wholesale vendors, they will send you gorgeous catalogs online or through the mail filled with every bike accessory you have ever asked for plus some you hadn't yet dreamed of. Some will be priced at tantalizing discounts if you order ten or more. You'll receive flyers from them showing closeouts that must be purchased within days, even if you don't need them. You'll imagine crowds of customers swarming in to buy all these shiny new things and you'll tell yourself that it's your duty to provide these wonderful products to all those future customers. Your wholesale orders will be on credit, so it will be dangerously easy to place orders. Without knowing it, you will have stepped into the Las Vegas casino of retail purchasing with every flashing light and buzzer a tantalizing ticket to debt and disaster.

The best way to avoid it is to start with your budget and work plan for the year. Just as with all your other program elements, purchasing must have a purpose within your work plan and a maximum amount to spend. The first year your center is open you'll have to meet the basics. Every product you purchase must fit your mission of serving the most disadvantaged people. Talk to folks in the area to find out what their most common needs are. These might be patch kits, new inner tubes or tires. Find out the common sizes and whether they need knobby or street tread tires. Locks are another important item because people who live on the margins rarely have secure places to store a bike. Racks and baskets for people to add to their bikes can solve their load carrying concerns. Lights are also vital. You'll also need to stock your repair area with common repair parts and specialty bike tools.

A tip on tool purchasing: don't buy common items like hammers and screwdrivers from your bike parts wholesalers. You'll find a better variety and likely better quality at local tool dealers. Personally, I like to start with shops that sell used tools, but if you try this, check carefully for wear and breaks. If you have the time, try announcing your wish list of tools to your community. Many could come in as donations.

Write up a shopping list of your most needed items for that year before opening any wholesale bike parts catalog. Then use the catalogs to add prices next to each item on this list. Stay focused. Don't let the pretty pictures seize control of your hand to add unnecessary items. Then total the prices to compare with your budget for the purchase. This rule will serve you well for every purchase you make.

Another rule: use as few wholesale vendors as possible; two or three at the most. This will simplify your paperwork and consolidate your orders, which can lead to price breaks and free shipping. It might take a few orders before you find the vendors that stock the items you need at the best prices and also offer great customer service. But as soon as you are familiar with them, choose the two best and stick to these for all your orders.

As you place more orders to replenish sold items you will begin to recognize your most popular products. Create a reorder system that keeps these products stocked all the time. As people purchase your products and services you will have more room for expanding your product offerings. At this point you'll want to start sorting your products into two roles to help control your purchasing:

1. Primary and expected products: these bring people in—keep them fully stocked at all times;

2. Profit generating add-ons: these are the eye candy, high profit items that people buy on impulse—add these with caution only when you have excess money for inventory, only buy inexpensive products, mark them up well above keystone, and stop ordering any that don't sell out quickly.

This leads me to the next big warning: if you delegate purchasing to another staff member, likely a manager, be sure this person is the *only* purchaser. Train them to follow the budgeted shopping list rule, then keep a close watch to ensure they are sticking to it and not spending money on unnecessary items. You can create an ordering system that any staff member can add to. This can be as simple as a pad of paper where they note their name and the needed item. The purchaser can then assess whether or not to add all these items and find ways to combine them to leverage quantity price breaks. Holding one person accountable for purchasing will keep orders under control and save your organization precious money.

Pricing is the other factor that ensures you sell what you purchase and reach your needed profit goal. Remember that even at keystone (fifty percent markup; covered earlier in this chapter) you will be lucky to make a one percent profit after all other expenses at your center are paid. So start with this pricing rule of doubling the wholesale cost you pay. But don't stop there. Research prices your competitors use. If a product cannot be keystoned without its price being well above a nearby competitor's price, consider dropping it from your lineup. And if no other retailer is carrying a product, go ahead and mark it as far above keystone as you dare. Customers expect to pay a substantial price for a quality product. If your price is lower than what they expected, they will perceive it as bad quality and won't buy it. I've heard of retailers raising the price of certain products until someone complained. That's how they knew they hit the right price just before that one. Once you determine the right price for all your products, stick to that price even if you score a discount from your wholesaler on one of your orders. The only time you should change a proven price is when your wholesaler raises their price and forces you to.

Pricing your refurbished bikes and used parts must follow these same concepts. Fully assess the total cost to your organization of every donated bike you take in. Note the amount of time and expense of announcing your need for donated bikes, working with the donor, accepting the bike, storing the bike, diagnosing the bike's repair needs, paying a master mechanic to fix and tune the bike to a high standard, paying for new and used parts installed, and setting aside showroom space to display it. Then assess the expected price of a similar used bike in your area. If you cannot sell the bike at a price that will fully cover all direct and indirect costs of that bike plus some profit, do not spend the time and expense on fixing it! Instead, tear it down for its usable parts.

Donated mass merchant bikes (I like the term "bicycle shaped objects" or "BSOs" for these) are one example where you will likely choose to tear down rather than rebuild. Their frames are made from poor quality metal and are not sturdy enough for your clients' transportation needs. Also, retail customers will know they can buy the same bike new for far less than you would have to charge. These bikes are built by underpaid, overworked disadvantaged people in countries that are willing to misuse their workers for economic gain. Amazingly, because these companies pay their workers so little, they can afford to outfit their bikes with some good parts you can use on other bikes such as tires, tubes, grips, seats, seat posts, nuts and bolts, and sometimes pedals. Discard the frames, forks, stems, handlebars and brakes because these are usually such poor quality they will not be safe to use on other bikes. Also discard the wheels of these bikes unless you or your master mechanic are sure they are unusually good quality because wheels on these bikes are prone to collapse. Find a scrap metal dealer in your area who deals with steel and aluminum. Often they will give you a surprising amount of money for all that metal.

Pricing used parts should also be straightforward. Find a comparable part in your vendor catalogs, note what the new price would be and then price the used part slightly below that price depending on its level of wear.

You might find that volunteers will enjoy tearing down donated bikes that cannot be refurbished. But remember that volunteers are not free! In order to engage volunteers in meaningful and useful work for your organization, you must invest significant time and money in planning for their duties, enlisting them, supervising them, feeding them, recording their accomplishments and thanking them. If a volunteer is set to work on a meaningless job or spends time on something that must be done over, this is money wasted. For instance, without supervision a volunteer might tear down a bike that was supposed to be refurbished. Another might misinterpret "tear down" and fully disassemble parts such as pedals and quality wheels, loosing small parts in the process. On top of such wasted money, consider that this volunteer could have spent that misused time actually bringing money into your organization through fundraising activities. So, if you use volunteers to tear down donated bikes, be sure to note their hourly time as an expense, roughly the same as the hourly wage of your entry level employees, and calculate that into the cost of your used bikes and parts.

Pricing is an art form that takes into account many different factors including customer expectations, customer convenience, perceived value, and the profit the product must generate to justify its taking up space in your center. As you do your own shopping, look for how other business folks markup and your tolerance level as their customer. Why do you pay ten dollars for popcorn at the movie theatre when you know the corn and container only cost a tenth of this price? When a drink vendor on a city street provides a cup and ice along with the can of soda, does this make you happy to pay a dollar and 25 cents even though you could have bought six warm cans at the convenience store around the corner for the same price? Your customers will also be calculating the convenience and service you and your staff offer along with your products. Keep this in mind as you price your products.

Training your sales staff and managers about pricing is critical even if you designate one manager to price products (giving your purchaser this duty will round out their understanding of the life of each product). Any staff member who helps customers must understand that sticking to the designated prices is critical, that there is no room for discounting. Show this by reminding them that a ten dollar discount takes one thousand dollars in extra product sales just to break even. Also explain that discounting sends the wrong message to customers and will train them to demand a discount. Your center will never compete with the mass merchant or online discount retailers. Remember the soda seller. You're offering your customers convenience and service the discounters can't.

You will have to go through a similar process to determine the right prices for your bicycle repair services as well as your career training fees. Set your hourly bicycle repair service rate to match or exceed what other bike shops are charging in your area. All of your service and training fees, just like your product fees, must be at or above comparable repair and training services in your area. Your micro lending and subsidy program will ensure that even your most impoverished customers can purchase these products and services at the very same retail price as everyone else. Find details on setting these up in Chapter 7.

Wholesale pricing won't come up until you are manufacturing bicycles and parts, have a surplus of refurbished bikes, *and* are supporting social bike shops from your center. Once you reach this point and are ready to support the graduates of your full career training program who want to open their own social bike shop, you will want to consider wholesale prices. By supplying these social bike shops with bikes and parts you will help the owners keep their shops stocked with the items their customers need. But just as with your retail pricing at your center, you must fully assess all of your costs of each item. Wholesale pricing must cover all of these costs and a bit of profit. You won't have to include storage or display costs or your cost of paying sales staff to sell the bikes and parts, so this will bring your wholesale price below your retail price. Since these social bike shop owners will be trained in bike repair, you can also supply them with surplus donated bikes for them to refurbish themselves. But you'll still have to charge them enough to cover the cost of the bike to your organization. Keep a tight control on your wholesale sales, ensuring that only your certified owners of social bike shops can purchase at these prices, and never reveal these prices to regular customers. Also note that these social bike shop owners will not pay sales tax on these wholesale purchases, but will have to charge sales tax when they sell them.

Inventory turns are another measure of the success of any retail business. An inventory turn happens when every product you purchased for resale has been sold. The most successful retailers enjoy many inventory turns each year. In the bicycle business, two turns each year is reason for celebration. Anything less than a full turn of your inventory in a year and you've become a storage unit for your own personal collection of rotting stuff rather than a retailer. This goes back to your purchasing. You've got to purchase only products that sell quickly. Your early orders are bound to include some mistakes. You need to get rid of any products that haven't sold in a year in order to keep your center's limited display space stocked with the products your customers need. You can track this by including a tiny date on all of your price tags (some pricing guns include this feature). Close-outs and product donations are the best way to go. Never allow confusion between close-outs and discounts with your staff. Place your close-out bin or table at the back of your show room so it doesn't send the message of discounting to your customers. The products in that bin need to look like you want to get rid of them, completely different from the professionally displayed products in your main displays. Obviously you want to keep close-outs to a bare minimum because each one cuts into your profits. But it's better to get rid of stale products that aren't selling than let them take up valuable space where new salable products can be displayed.

Controlling inventory through careful purchases that lead to full inventory turns will ensure that the retail part of your center is profitable. While your purchaser might seem to have a tight handle on all your products, taking a full inventory always reveals surprises. Taking inventory means to count every single product in your store that's for sale and record the price you paid for it (not the retail price). You and your staff will have to take a full inventory at least once a year, at the end of each year for your tax paperwork. This is because your cost of any product that hasn't been sold must be removed from a line item on your tax form called "cost of goods sold." That existing inventory remains as an asset to your organization until it is sold. Even though you will only be required to take full inventory once each year, consider doing it halfway through the year just to get a full picture of your inventory, pull out products that should be closed out, and to discover salable products that have been shoved into dark corners out of sight from customers.

One way to recall the importance of inventory control is to imagine every product as encasing a stack of money in the amount your organization had to pay for it. If a box of inner tubes has been pushed behind a work bench, think of it instead as a box of money that can only be accessed through customer purchases. Now, wouldn't it be better to unpack those tubes so they can be sold to customers? Same goes for disorganized, cluttered or dimly lit displays. If customers walk right by your products, those metaphorical stacks of money might as well be hidden in a back room. Taking inventory is one of the best ways of finding and remedying hidden or badly displayed products. You and your staff should also keep a vigilant lookout for this sort of thing and make corrections right away.

One last note on inventory: once you move into manufacturing bicycles and parts for sale, you will need to include in your annual inventory the materials you used as well as the labor costs you paid to create these products. This is a bit more complex than taking inventory of products you simply purchased from your vendors. Work with your accountant on this to ensure you use the correct figures.

Merchandising and Displays

Merchandising is another art form that you and your staff will have to master in order to make your center profitable. Unless products are displayed well, they simply will not sell. No customer is going to dig to the bottom of a pile of bike seats. No one will look through a box of stuff on the floor. Only products that are displayed between waist height and eyelevel where they are easy to touch will capture the attention of your customers.

Another important merchandising concept is called "white space." This simply means leaving a space around every product on display. If five locks are displayed on a shelf in a pile, you might as well have never unpacked them from the shipment. Move them apart to leave a space between each so your customers will see five different locks rather than an indiscernible mess. Display hooks that hold several of the same product can retain white space while allowing your staff to keep popular items well stocked.

Your floor plan is also vital to your merchandising success. Many studies of retail customers have confirmed that most customers turn right after entering a retail store. It's true! I've tested this on myself and watched my own customers. Set your showroom up to tap this and cause most of your customers to have a full tour of your store before they reach what they came in for. The more they see, the more they are likely to buy. Place your specialty items to the right and your most popular, expected products far to the left. This includes your close-outs that should be in the back on the left side. Never put your counter to the right because customers will head directly for it, ask your staff person there to fetch what they need and never see another item in your showroom.

Set your displays up so customers can see to the end of each even from the front door. Place complimentary items together so that customers looking for one item will remember they need another. For instance, place your tire levers next to your tires for customers ready to do their own tire change. Have fun with your displays. You can add creative props or interactive ways for your customers to try out products. Be sure that every product is well lit, well dusted and none are left in the shadows.

Don't forget outside displays that will grab the attention of passersby, especially bicycles or other large items. Stick to large items because they are easy to lock to avoid theft. You can also add eye-catching landscaping and displays of art as long as it is professional, not junky. Outside furniture that welcomes people to linger will also draw attention because people are drawn to people. A portable sandwich board sign placed each day near the street can be useful for announcing events, training classes and close-outs to grab people who might have gone past otherwise. Even if you do announce your close-outs on such a sign, never place the actual items outside. This diminishes the perception of your center. Keep these items in the back so even customers who come in only for the close-outs have to take a full tour of your showroom.

Customer Service and Sales

Great customer service and sales at your center will require more staff training than at most retail and service establishments because your primary customers come from the margins of your community. From your early work developing your program you will have learned about some of their special needs, language and word choices that set them at ease, and what they most need from your program. The best way to ensure your staff members are sensitive to these important details is to hire disadvantaged people from the neighborhood. Even so, you will still have to constantly reinforce these concepts to ensure that every disadvantaged area resident who enters your center feels like royalty. Customer service and sales is a skill that takes years to master even for the most talented employees.

While your center will also welcome regular retail customers, it must have more layers of offerings than other retail establishments. This will require your sales staff to be even better at finding out what each customer or client needs. Someone might come in asking for a bike, but after a calm and respectful conversation, your staff member might discover that they are a perfect candidate for career training as well.

Sales staff training starts with their first week on the job. During their first week you will have to cover all the employee policies, organization principles and basic details of their job along with sales and service concepts. Introduce them to every product and service your center offers including program services in career training and job search. Include details of your center's bike repair services such as the hourly service rate, the difference between piecemeal repairs and a full tune up, and so on.

You'll also need to cover payment details such as what info to gather from customers who pay by check or credit card and how your micro lending and subsidy program works for qualifying customers.

Obviously cash is the best way to receive payments, but many customers prefer to pay by check or credit card. For checks, the danger is returned checks, which is why noting info from driver's licenses or picture ID cards is vital so you can find customers who bounce checks.

Taking physical credit cards is a bit of work to set up, but worth it in the end. Many customers expect to pay with a credit card, so even though you will be charged extra fees for each credit card purchase, realize that the purchase likely wouldn't have occurred if you hadn't been able to accept the credit card. This also means that stolen or altered credit cards will cross your counter. Work with your bank to set up a secure system and train your staff to gather all pertinent information to protect your organization from credit card fraud. Also, do not allow your staff to accept credit cards over the phone as this is the most common way for criminals to use stolen credit cards. Purchase your credit card terminal rather than leasing it as this will save your organization lots of money in the long term.

Once your physical credit card acceptance system is set up, you can connect your website's credit card system to it. If you had started with PayPal or a similar service, this shift will keep your online donors from having to leave your website to donate. Work with your web designer to set up a proven online credit card encryption system that displays common assurances of security to your donors such as the yellow padlock and familiar security systems.

Make your micro lending program the only credit program you offer. Never extend credit to retail customers. The beauty of accepting credit cards is that you can still work with customers who need credit in order to buy, but the responsibility of getting payment shifts to the credit card company.

As you move through training, ask your new staff member questions about what you've covered as you go along rather than burying them in endless information. If they aren't grasping important details, go over them again.

When you get to sales training, spend quality time explaining these important concepts:

1) Greet everyone who enters the center within 15 seconds. This makes people feel welcome and encourages them to linger.

2) Engage the customer in conversation and never ask yes or no questions. Teach your sales staff that their job is to learn from the customer what they came in for and offer ways your organization can help them. Yes or no questions kill any chance of this interaction because they are usually answered with the dreaded "No, just looking." Have your staff practice respectful conversation starters that have something to do with the customer such as noting their unusual bike or asking how they managed

to walk there in such hot weather. Also have them practice getting past the "No, just looking" response in case of slips.

3) Once trust is established, find out what they need. The step right before this is an important buffer. Imagine if you walked into a store and the first question a sales representative asked you amounted to, "What do you want?" Major turn off. Train your staff to ease into casual conversation and then, within just a few minutes, to shift into finding out what they need. Remind your staff that everyone who walks in the door wants to either buy something or sign up for your services. If they leave without doing so, something went wrong in the conversation.

4) Narrow the choices to two or three. Here is where your staff's familiarity with the products and services is vital. They must be able to translate what the customer tells them into pertinent suggestions that fit the customer's needs and keep the choices to a maximum of three, two is better. Too many choices will just confuse the customer and might scare them away.

5) Connect features to the customer's needs. Train your sales staff to not only describe features of a product or service, but show the customer how that feature will benefit them. I've always found the phrase "so that you" to be an excellent reminder of this. I learned to never point out a product's feature unless I could use this phrase. For instance, compare these two sales pitches:

- "This bike comes with alloy rims."
- "This bike comes with double wall aluminum alloy rims that are lighter and stronger than steel *so that you* can lift your bike easier and not have to worry about bent wheels."

There are many variations of the phrase, so they don't have to use it exactly. Make sure your sales staff understand this concept, though, otherwise they risk making the customer feel stupid, which is likely to send them packing.

6) Close the sale with an add-on. In most retail businesses, this means asking the customer if they are ready to purchase the product, waiting for the answer and, if it is affirmative, suggesting one more, lower priced product that would be a nice addition to the main product. Add-ons must be quite different than the main product and lower priced to avoid making the customer second guess their decision. For instance, a customer who has decided to buy a bike might appreciate a suggestion of a lock so that they can ride their bike right away to run errands and not worry about it being stolen. At your center, this concept will be the same, but your

staff will have to have a much broader view of "add-ons." For instance, a discussion with a customer may have focused entirely on a bike, but they may have offered a few hints about needing a job. Your sales staff can then suggest that after they've finalized their bike purchase they should meet with a program staff member to add their name to your job search services.

By training your sales staff in these six important steps to successful sales, you will ensure that everyone who comes to your center is well served. Practicing at your center will help your staff refine their sales skills. I also highly recommend sending them out into your community to test the concepts at other retail stores. Ask them to play roles of different types of customers to see how the sales people respond. Have them pronounce the dreaded "No, just looking" and see if the sales person bothers to re-engage them in conversation.

Remember that the benefits of great service do not remain secrets to your happy customers. Each of them has the potential of becoming your center's most important marketing tool because they will tell others about their exceptional experience at your center. This also goes for bad experiences, which is why constant training and reinforcement of these sales concepts with your staff are vital. A customer or client will never forget how their experience at your center made them feel. One of my favorite quotes in this regard comes from Maya Angelou: "*I've learned that people will forget what you said, people will forget what you did, but people will never forget how you made them feel.*" Do whatever you can to make everyone who comes to your center feel like royalty.

Branding, Marketing and Promotion

I've already discussed the need to choose a great name for your organization and to register it before opening your center. But your concern over your organization's name and image only starts there. You and your entire team must understand the concept of branding and setting your center out as uniquely valuable to your community. Potential customers, partners and donors have to hear or see a name repeatedly before they will feel comfortable engaging with it. Such impressions can be delivered through media; discussions with friends; a visit to a website; noticing a sign, a sticker, a T-shirt, anything that includes the brand—name, logo, colors and tagline—of the organization.

I've heard that it can take up to 27 brand impressions (i.e., viewing a logo or name) before someone takes action because so many of these impressions are coupled with distractions or bad timing. Think of this the next time you encounter an ad for something you just barely recognize and ask yourself how many times you've seen it before. Then ask how many times you'll need to see it again before you purchase that product or service. How many times did you have to see or hear about Facebook before you went to that website and filled in the two simple boxes for free? Branding to convince people to travel to a place to make a purchase or donation has to be even more effective than Facebook. And every one of these 27 impressions must give the identical name, logo, colors and tagline, otherwise they do not count. I have come across too many organization marketing schemes that look nothing like their websites. Some leaders of organizations with long, institutional names shorten them for promotions or turn them into acronyms in order to make them more appealing. This detaches the promotion from all other impressions of the organization.

The best way to control the branding of your organization is to create what is often called a corporate identity manual. Include in this manual the exact dimensions of your organization's logo, the exact brand colors using common color codes such as the Pantone Matching System (PMS) or CMYK, the exact wording of your tagline, and rules for the use of all of these components. These corporate identity manuals are usually just a few pages long, but clearly spell out these dimensions, colors and usages. Search the internet to find countless corporate identity manuals as examples.

Beyond these core branding elements, the message development of all your promotions must follow strict guidelines as well in order to avoid confusion. Once your corporate identity manual is complete, designate just one staff member as spokesperson. This person will be responsible for approving all promotional materials and speaking to members of the media. This person must be well versed in appropriate message development and understand messages to avoid. For instance, it would be quite easy for an untrained staff member to describe your center as a charity for poor people. Such misrepresentation would at best confuse people and at worst set in place a damaging reputation that could take years to overcome.

Even with a spokesperson designated, train all of your staff, volunteers and board members to clearly articulate proper messages about your organization and center. Practice an "elevator speech" with them—a few sentences that capture the work of your organization that could be delivered in a quick elevator ride with a prospective donor or partner. Give this to your team in writing and post it on your website for easy reference. Underscore the gravity of improper messages and misuse of branding materials. Cover the rules of use, including referring all media representatives to the spokesperson, and that the rules will be strictly enforced.

Once you're ready to get the word out, free promotion is always best because people will know it's authentic. Avoid paying for advertising. Paid advertisements are so pervasive and absurd these days, people have learned to ignore them so it's like throwing money away. Focus instead on these cost-free methods of getting the word out:

- <u>Press releases</u> – capture exciting successes and upcoming events in concise press releases. Send them to all print, radio and TV media. Post them to social media sites to catch more readers and encourage forwarding. Find a template on One Street's website under Media in the left menu.
- <u>Partner with like-minded organizations</u> – team up for fun events and share your promotions networks. These partners can also help you reach more disadvantaged people and introduce them to your organization.
- <u>E-newsletters</u> – email these out once a month to your constantly growing list of fans. Include news of your organization's accomplishments as well as information that is useful to readers. Post them to social media sites to increase readership and encourage forwarding.
- <u>Website</u> – always keep your website updated and add news items to the home page. All promotions including press releases and e-newsletters must include your organization's website address and send people back to it so they can engage even more with your programs.
- <u>Word of mouth</u> – This is the best free promotion you could hope for. Your current customers and clients are the best potentials for spreading it, so make sure your merchandising, sales and customer service are excellent for everyone who walks in the door.

Bookkeeping, Collecting Sales Tax and Reporting

Ah, the delightful topic of bookkeeping. You've likely noted the many benefits of great bookkeeping, especially staying on top of your profit and loss situation. By understanding your books, you and your team can make those fine adjustments that spell the difference between success and failure in business.

Your most important component of your bookkeeping system, at least at the beginning, is your accountant. This person might be the pro bono accountant you worked with for your nonprofit registration or they might be a different accountant who is more versed in business management. If you have chosen the nonprofit organization structure, find an accountant who not only understands business bookkeeping, but nonprofits as well so they can help you analyze your social business in the context of your nonprofit organization structure. Ask other nonprofit leaders and business owners to recommend an accountant. Before hiring an accountant, meet with them to ensure you are comfortable working with them and that they can translate accounting lingo into everyday language. The best accountant in the world would be useless to you if the way they explain your books sounds like a foreign language. Your accountant can help you set up your accounting system and decipher the information it reveals. You will need to pay this person for their services, but in the end, it will be money well spent.

Note that bookkeeping and accounting are different activities. Bookkeeping is the act of recording all income and expenses. You and your managers must take careful care of your center's bookkeeping so that everything will be recorded accurately. I do not recommend hiring an outside bookkeeper. Such a person would lack the detailed understanding of your center's operations necessary to ensure the books reflect actual activity. Also, anyone who does the books for your center will have the opportunity to embezzle money, but outside contractors have fewer ties to your organization than salaried staff members. Even if you ask a trusted manager to do the books each day, check their work regularly and ensure that deposits into your organization's bank account match income. By keeping your bookkeeping as close to you as possible, you will remove the temptation to embezzle your center's hard-earned money.

Accounting, on the other hand, is the process of organizing the information captured through bookkeeping into reports that are useful for you and your team and meet tax reporting requirements. You will likely need your accountant's help with payroll and will definitely need their help with your year-end tax preparation.

For Social Bike Business programs in the U.S., I recommend using QuickBooks for your bookkeeping and accounting system software because it is commonly used by accountants. If you are not in the U.S., ask accountants in your area which accounting software they'd recommend. In fact, accounting software is not much different from paper bookkeeping ledgers that business owners have used for centuries, so if computers are a problem in your area, paper ledgers might work fine. The problem with only using paper ledgers is that you will still need to total all the columns of numbers in order to analyze your business results. A combination of daily paper ledgers and input to your computer might be a useful system. Paper ledgers will likely be enough for many of the social bike shops and other small businesses your center helps start, but your organization and Social Bike Business program will be complex enough that software will become necessary.

If you can't afford a nice accounting software like QuickBooks right away, a spreadsheet that comes with your computer such as Excel or the free version from OpenOffice will suffice until you can. At least with such a spreadsheet you can easily add columns and pull out sections of data to analyze. Keep in mind that an investment in QuickBooks or similar software will pay you back immediately in time saved and the quality of accounting reports produced, so make this purchase as soon as you possibly can. In the U.S., there are several software sellers that offer deep discounts on QuickBooks for 501(c)(3) nonprofits. Start by checking Techsoup.org. If that doesn't work, do an internet search for nonprofit software discounts.

Before setting up your software (even paper ledgers or a

spreadsheet), sit down with your accountant to determine which line items to include in your income and expense sections. Include just enough to cover all your common income categories and expense items. These will include income and expenses for both your center and your whole organization. So make sure your center's line items can be easily pulled out and analyzed separately much like they should be in your budgeting and cash flow systems covered earlier in this chapter. By aligning your bookkeeping system, which records your exact income and expenses, with your budget estimates you will get the most out of your budgeting system. Keeping your center's income and expenses on separate lines will allow you to create its own profit and loss statements. Too many or too few line items will make your reports impossible to decipher. By creating a quality system from the start, you will save significant time in the future.

One important note here: avoid creating or using an expense line item called "miscellaneous" because it is too tempting to record receipts there. Not only is a miscellaneous line item useless for analysis, it looks suspicious with any significant amount. By carefully including enough expense lines that capture all your common expenses, you will avoid the need for a miscellaneous line.

Record all of your center's income daily. Cash registers can be handy for this because even the most basic model allows you to categorize products and services that match your bookkeeping system. Each time your staff rings up an item for sale, they also hit a code key for its particular category. At the end of each day, your staff can "close out" the register, which produces a printout report for the day. They can then enter all of the totals per category into your paper ledger or directly onto your computer's bookkeeping system.

I recommend that even if you use a cash register, also use sequentially numbered paper receipts with carbonless copies for all of your transactions. I learned the hard way that such a backup system is vital because a cash register is just a machine, bound to hiccup. Without a paper receipt backup, all of your day's sales records can easily be lost. Customers also like to receive an itemized receipt rather than a mysterious, coded cash register receipt. This is particularly true for bicycle repair jobs to show exactly what your mechanics did. Either have these double-copy, carbonless receipt pads printed with your organization's name at the top or get a rubber stamp made so your staff can stamp each receipt. Each evening when you or your manager does the books, check that all receipts in the numbered sequence are there, even voided receipts, and that these receipts match the cash register record for the day. This will ensure that no one is misusing receipts to circumvent the cash register and steal customer money.

One more important note about handwritten receipts: require your staff to always note the date, *including the year*, on every receipt. If you ever have to find a bookkeeping problem by looking back through receipts, the date is critical. If there is no year noted and several years of receipts got jumbled in one box, you will have an unimaginable headache on your hands. Also, including the date with the year will help your customers who need to keep their receipt for their records.

There are some very expensive point-of-sale (POS) computer systems that work like a cash register and enter the data directly to your computer's bookkeeping system. Once your center hits the big time you can consider adding a POS system. But remember that even with such a fancy system, this is still a two step process of entering the day's sales then transferring the data into the bookkeeping and accounting system.

Deposit all cash and checks into your organization's bank account daily. This prevents theft and will ensure that checks that were written on dwindling bank accounts are covered before the customer's money runs out.

Record all of your expenses in your organization's check register. The best way to do this is to pay bills and buy supplies with checks. A debit card can work, too, but a check will give you more information if you have to look up the expense later. Avoid using credit cards because they will tempt you to spend money your organization does not have (re-read the section on cash flow and plan ahead instead). Also business credit card fees and interest are higher than personal credit cards and can siphon untold amounts of money you could otherwise have used for your programs. Another thing to avoid is auto-bill-paying services because you will lose control of your expenses and miss recording them promptly. Never pay bills or buy major supplies with cash because you won't have a backup record of the expense.

Petty cash is a useful system for taking care of minor supply purchases that will keep your center operating efficiently. You don't want your staff to have to find you or a manager every time a necessary supply runs out. But limit petty cash to only a small amount and keep a very strict recording system. A small safe or lockable box will work well. Write a check for fifty dollars to "CASH" at your bank and record the check as "petty cash." Get this cash in small bills. Place it inside the secure box with a record sheet that starts with fifty dollars (or close to that amount in your currency) and includes a table with at least four columns for: name, items bought, amount and date. Each time a staff person runs to the store for an urgent supply, they must record the purchase and place the receipt in the box. If the money remaining does not match the record, require that your manager, or whoever you place in charge of the petty cash, to replenishes the missing money with their own. This should underscore their responsibility for keeping a close watch on it. Once the petty cash is nearly spent, remove the record sheet and receipts, record them in your bookkeeping system and file them in your records. Then start the process over with a new fifty dollars of cash and a fresh record sheet.

You will also need to balance your organization's checkbook every month. No matter how careful you are recording income and expenses, there are too many opportunities to make mistakes. Your bank will send a monthly statement that shows everything that went through their system. Carefully compare their final numbers with yours. If the numbers don't match perfectly, go through every item until you find the mistake and correct it. Then mark that month as balanced so that you only have to examine the next month when the next bank statement arrives.

There are several categories of income and expenses you will have to understand and differentiate from each other in your bookkeeping system:

- Product sales income (several line items to help your inventory control)
- Service income, including repair and training fees (usually one line item)
- Recurring supply expenses (can use several lines)
- Inventory expense (always one line item)
- One-time equipment expenses, also known as capital (one line item)

In the U.S. and most other countries, product sales may require sales tax to be collected. Check with your local government to find out. You can have as many line items in your cash register and bookkeeping system for product sales as you like, but keep them to the absolute minimum required for you to fully analyze your sales. Once you set up your cash register with sales-taxed categories for products and one untaxed category for service, it will note the sales tax collected separately. Also make sure your staff note sales tax collected on a separate line on every receipt they fill out.

You are not required to collect sales tax on service income. Check with your government to be sure. This is why service must be noted as a separate income line item in your bookkeeping system.

Understanding the difference between sales tax and income tax is vital to all business operators. Your nonprofit organization should by now be structured to allow exemption from income tax on all your center's sales because those sales are "substantially related" to your organization's mission. If your organization ever does sell items that are not substantially related to its mission, you will simply need to record this income separately on your annual tax form and pay that tax at the end of that year. But nonprofits may or may not be exempt from collecting and paying sales tax. Check with your local or national government to be sure.

If needed, your accountant and local government officials can help you set up your sales tax account when you register your center as a local business. Your local government will send you a form on a regular schedule, most likely monthly. You'll use this form to fill in the amount of sales tax you collected during that period and then send it in with your check for that amount. Very simple, as long as you have set up your bookkeeping system to pull out this amount.

Include expense line items for your common supply purchases such as for cleaning, trainings, office work and repair service. Include a separate line item for one-time equipment purchases such as computers, welding machines, desks, tables and chairs. These will be recorded as capital assets for your organization.

Inventory expense is what you pay for the products you will sell. Until you start manufacturing bikes and parts, this number should be easy to find straight from your wholesale vendor receipts. Once you start manufacturing, work with your accountant to determine the cost of each of these products you sell, including what you paid your staff to manufacture them. Note that in the U.S., you will not pay sales tax on your wholesale purchases. Sales tax is only collected for the final retail sale to the end customer. If your country uses the value-added-tax (VAT) system, you might also have to pay this tax to your wholesaler. Because of this, as well as the need to differentiate the money you spend on inventory from supplies, inventory must be separated from other expenses in your bookkeeping system.

Keep all your records, bank statements and receipts as long as you have room to store them. If you must throw some away, note that in the U.S. you are required to keep your bank statements and receipts for a minimum of three years. But never throw away your organization's bookkeeping records or tax paperwork.

Once your bookkeeping system is set up and you've gotten into the swing of it you'll find it is not as difficult as it might seem now. The most important thing to remember about bookkeeping is that it is in fact simple. Business owners have been keeping their books for centuries in the exact same form as today's most sophisticated accounting software. All it requires is an accurate way to record every transaction of your business from both the income and expense side, then arrange these numbers to allow the owner (and, yes, the government) to see a clear picture of how the business is doing. Keep this concept of simplicity in mind no matter how you set up your first bookkeeping system and you will ensure that your organization can track its Social Bike Business program with ease.

For further reading on business bookkeeping concepts, I have never found a better book than *Small Time Operator: How to Start Your Own Business, Keep Your books, Pay Your Taxes, and Stay out of Trouble*, by Bernard B. Kamoroff, CPA. I was fortunate to discover it just as I was opening my bike shop in 1991. It is now in its 12th edition and remains one of the most popular books available on starting a small business. While it includes lots of details particular to the U.S., any novice small business owner around the world will find invaluable wisdom throughout. You might even consider using it as a textbook in your career training program.

Insurance, Warranties and Other Legal Requirements

The number one rule of insurance is to buy only what you need. This doesn't mean skipping insurance. That could set your organization up for disaster. Rather, you and your team need to fully assess the risks that threaten your organization and center. These can include fire, theft, property liability (if a customer hurts themselves at your center), product liability (once you start manufacturing), and bike rental liability (if you add this to your income generators). Discuss each one thoroughly amongst yourselves so you understand the level of risk. Fire could destroy the building and all of your equipment. How much would it cost to rebuild? Can you afford to pay a lower premium and risk only partial coverage? If there's no fire, this could save your organization thousands of dollars over the years. But if there is a fire... Go through the same discussion for theft and liability. These internal discussions are important *before* you visit an insurance agent because that insurance agent's job is to scare the hell out of you so you will buy as much insurance as he or she can sell you. Stay focused and only buy what you need.

I also recommend getting several quotes before deciding on your final insurance policy. When I first started renting bikes at my bike shop and had to add this type of insurance, I learned more than I ever wanted to know about the insurance industry. Insurance brokers are nothing more than a bunch of gamblers. And if they don't understand the activity you need insured, they are going to charge you the maximum rate. In the end, I found an insurance company that covered bike shops and understood the low level risk of bike rentals. In fact, by switching to them, I ended up cutting my bill from what my original insurance provider was charging for the same coverage without the bike rentals. Talk to local bike shop owners to find out which insurance companies they use and whether they are happy with their coverage and premiums. Also check with bike shop associations that serve your area to see if they recommend any insurance companies. In the U.S., that would be the National Bicycle Dealers Association www.nbda.com and in Europe, it's the European Twowheel Retailers' Association www.etra-eu.com.

A different category of insurance you may need to purchase covers employee injuries. In the U.S., this is called Workers Compensation Insurance. It's required by law in the U.S. and is provided by companies that specialize in this coverage. If, like the U.S., your country does not have universal healthcare, this sort of insurance may be required by law. But even if it is not, consider providing it anyway because you want to provide a supportive work place for your employees.

Warranties are another management concern that you will have to learn. Every manufacturer of the products you provide will have some sort of warranty system that will allow your customers to return products for a full refund if a defect is found. Before allowing your staff to issue a refund for any warranties, set a strict policy that they must follow. Most importantly, they must check the exact wording of the manufacturer's warranty. There is always a time limit, so they must check the date on the customer's receipt (here's another vital reason for including dates with the year on every receipt). Some manufacturers require proof of a defect during manufacture. Just because a product is broken doesn't mean it was defective. A call to the manufacturer to confirm that the warranty will be covered is also a good idea. Adherence to your policy is critical because if you send that product back after the warranty expires or without clear proof of a defect, the manufacturer will not send you a refund and your organization will lose that money. If the customer has no receipt or there is no manufacturer's warranty to be found, do not issue a refund. Then consider dropping that product from your lineup.

Once you start manufacturing your own bikes and parts I recommend developing a warranty for these products. This will elevate the perception of your products in your customers' minds and build confidence in your products. A warranty tells customers that you will stand behind the quality of your products.

There may be other legal requirements or expectations of businesses in your area. Check with your pro bono attorney, local business owners and government officials to ensure you have met all the requirements to make your bicycle community center an upstanding and respected business in your community.

Now that you've set up all these important management systems, you are ready to watch your center come to life. As you move ahead, much of the initial system set up will have to be adapted and adjusted to fully meet the needs of your center, especially in the first two years of operation. These adjustments and the lessons you learn from them will be invaluable material to add to your career training program. They will give you and your trainers real life stories that show your students why such systems are vital for the success of their own business. And as you teach your career training students these lessons, their ideas and questions will help you refine your center's operations. No for-profit business can lay claim to such an effective feedback and upgrade system. So remember its value and keep tapping your training program for inspirations.

Once your center is hopping and, after studying your profit and loss statements, you and your team can confidently claim that your center is profitable, it might be time to look at expanding your program offerings. The next section will help you add new program elements including the support of social bike shops and manufacturing of bikes and parts. The last chapter will dabble in even more creative ways of serving the bicycle needs of marginalized folks and adding new income generation opportunities to your center.

Section
3

Expanding
Your Program

CHAPTER 10

Supporting Social Bike Shops

Once you have established your bicycle community center and it is running smoothly, one of the best ways to expand your Social Bike Business program is by supporting disadvantaged people who want to start their own social bike shop to serve their neighbors. This support should include your continued coaching and assistance as they build their business as well as helping them stock their shop with bikes and parts obtained through your program. Not only will this help these budding new business owners, their shop will play a key role in your program by reaching farther into distressed neighborhoods to bring bicycling to many more disadvantaged people. As I mentioned earlier, one of the top complaints I've heard from local leaders around the world is that distressed neighborhoods are not served by bike shops. People who live in these neighborhoods might find a way to get a bike, perhaps through your center, but if it breaks down, there will likely be no place for them to go to get it repaired within walking distance. This predicament can remove bicycling from their transportation options completely.

By supporting social bike shops that are owned and operated by graduates of all six of your career training modules you will be advancing two priority principles of Social Bike Business at once—providing career opportunities to disadvantaged people and establishing bike shops that serve the residents of distressed neighborhoods.

Even so, you will want to ensure that every social bike shop owner you support operates their shop to the highest standards. Consider the time you and your staff will spend to help them make their business run smoothly and, while they will pay your wholesale price for bikes and parts, this will still add to the administration expense of your organization. You will have to plan for this in your annual budget and raise the funds to pay for the staff and overhead costs of this work. So you must be confident that their shop is contributing to your organization's goal of serving the bicycling needs of the most disadvantaged people in your community.

Although their shop will be structured as a for-profit business, they must focus on social needs. Just as you have had to take extra care with your center to ensure it welcomes people from the margins of your community, their social bike shop must take similar care to do the same. The bikes and parts they offer must be sturdy, affordable and focused on transportation, not sport bikes. These owners must also prioritize serving their disadvantaged neighbors above profits. And their bike shop must be located where it is convenient for these priority customers to reach, in easy walking distance along a safe route. Any profits above a market salary for the owner must go into expanding the social bike shop to better serve the needs of marginalized people. If they expand to the point of needing to hire staff, they must hire impoverished people from the neighborhood and pay them a market rate salary.

In order to ensure that the bike shops you support through your program continue to meet all of these criteria, you must provide annual certification. This should include assessment of each bike shop's financial records, praise and complaints from its customers, and an inspection by you or one of your managers with a simple checklist for each criterion like:

☐ Bike shop is located in easy walking distance for residents of distressed neighborhoods;

☐ Bike shop is open at least five days a week during normal business hours;

☐ Bike shop clearly prioritizes disadvantaged neighborhood residents through promotions and direct contact with them;

☐ Bike shop's exterior and interior are clean, orderly and professional in appearance;

☐ Bikes and parts sold at the shop are of high quality, focused on transportation and affordable for area residents;

☐ Bike shop does not carry imported new bikes, new sport racing bikes or sell high-end sport bike accessories;

☐ If the shop has employees, they were living in or near poverty when hired and are paid a market salary for the area;

☐ Owner receives only a market rate salary comparable to other small business owners in the area;

☐ All profits are invested in the expansion of the social bike shop to better serve the needs of disadvantaged people.

If they fail on any of these or their financial records concern you, give them a chance to make a change within a reasonable time period. Offer guidance and assistance. But if they still don't qualify, you must remove them from your program support so it can go toward social bike shops that are serving your organization's mission.

Another important consideration is to never endorse the placement of a social bike shop in a neighborhood already served by a bike shop whose owner is proud to serve the disadvantaged area residents. Such bike shops are rare and we sure don't want to compete with them or cause them harm.

Many of the graduates of your career training program will scoff at all these requirements. Others might qualify for your support to start out, but then discover they prefer to work for profits with sport bicycles. This is fine. In fact, the world needs more for-profit bike shops, too. Offer some final words of advice and wish them the best of luck.

Those who qualify will have to give up easy profits from selling sport bikes and parts to rich people, but in return you can offer them a very nice package of support services:

- Promotion as one of the certified social bike shops supported by your program;
- Certification materials for that year that promote their shop as a social bike shop including a window sticker and a framed certificate for each year they qualify;

- Assistance with obtaining business loans to get started or expand;
- Assistance with qualifying individuals for subsidies and micro loans;
- Coordination of subsidies and micro loans to qualified individuals to purchase a bike, parts and repair service;
- With approval of wholesale vendors, combining parts orders to save on shipping costs and leveraging bulk discounts;
- First pick of the bikes donated at your center for them to refurbish themselves;
- First pick of bikes and parts refurbished and manufactured at your center, which they can purchase from your center at the wholesale price; and
- Coaching and guidance on business management.

Each social bike shop owner will have to go through all the business registration and permit processes you had to before opening your center. First, just like when you founded your organization, they will need their own business name, business address (post office box is fine), their own bank account, their own licenses and insurance. Once they find an appropriate location they can afford, they will go through much the same process as you and your team did before moving into your center. Since they will likely start off as sole proprietors (review the benefits of sole proprietorship for bike shops in Chapter 3), they will simply have to follow the business registration processes required for your area such as:

- Business license
- Business name registration
- Zoning qualifications
- Fire inspection
- Sign permit
- Certificate of occupancy
- Liability insurance
- Sellers permit and sales tax registration
- Utility deposits and upgrades to bring building up to code

You will recognize this list from Chapter 6 when I discussed requirements for opening your center. Even though you will have likely opened your center as part of a nonprofit organization, these requirements will be the same, so your experience will help you guide these novice business owners. You will be familiar with the staff and processes at each agency responsible for the requirements in your area. You may even choose to go along with your client to ensure the process goes smoothly so they can open their social bike shop as soon as possible.

One difference between social bike shops and your organization, at least in the U.S., is that when they are asked for their employer identification number (EIN), they will use their social security number rather than a number issued during incorporation. This is because they will be a sole proprietor rather than a corporation.

To ensure every new social bike shop owner you and your organization commit to supporting can reference pertinent legal requirements, consider providing each with a pamphlet or book that covers these for your area. For social bike shops in the U.S., I have to repeat my recommendation of the book *Small Time Operator: How to Start Your Own Business, Keep Your books, Pay Your Taxes, and Stay out of Trouble*, by Bernard B. Kamoroff, CPA.

Now that you have a handle on supporting social bike shops we can move on to one of the most popular concepts of the Social Bike Business program: manufacturing bikes and parts at your center.

CHAPTER 11

Manufacturing Social Bikes & Parts

ocal manufacture of bicycles has been the ultimate (though always optional) goal of the Social Bike Business program since its beginning because it targets the very core of the problem that has made the program necessary. Starting with the industrial revolution and continuing right through the 1970s, sturdy, affordable bicycles built for transportation were common in countries around the world. As the bike industry has shifted to sport bicycling and only manufacturing transportation bikes for rich people, the majority of the world's population has been left with junk. By guiding our local partners into successful manufacturing of bicycles, we are giving them the ability to build bikes that serve the needs of the struggling people they serve.

However, the resulting bicycles are only a small part of why manufacture is so important to the program. From the broader view, local bike manufacture avoids the harm inherent in outsourcings. For-profit bike companies must seek out the cheapest labor they can find to manufacture their bikes because they have a monetary bottom line. They have no reason to inquire into the labor practices of the countries they outsource to. As long as the factory tour gave them a good impression, they will have no problem convincing themselves that paying master welders less than a dollar an hour is good business. I actually had a CEO of bicycle company tell me with complete sincerity that the best way to get bikes manufactured for the Social Bike Business program is outsourcing *because* he only has to pay welders that build his frames sixty cents an hour! He made absolutely no connection between the impoverished people the program aims to help and the welders building his frames.

In comparison, if you and your team are ready to take this on, your center can manufacture high quality steel frames and pay your master welders up to ten dollars an hour to produce the bikes your clients need. Welding your own frames won't remove all the exploitation from the bikes you produce because many of the parts you use will still come from exploitive factories. But it will remove it from the frame production, painting and bike assembly, which make up the majority of the time that goes into creating a bike. As soon as the paint dries and the bike is assembled it can roll out the front door and into the waiting hands of one of your most deserving neighbors. Steel delivered to the back rolls out the front as a bike. No cardboard, no shipping, no export/import duties, no administration of the outsourcing process or travel costs. Just one neighbor making a great bike for another. By avoiding all these shipping and outsourcing costs and eliminating the bicycle wholesale vendor, even when you pay good wages you should manage to manufacture bikes that you can price at retail for 250 dollars or less at full keystone of your direct costs.

Now, as I mentioned earlier, ten dollars an hour is still far too low for a master welder, which leads to another major benefit of the program— training welders until they reach the master level and then launching them out of the program into a well-paying job. If you have set up your career training program efficiently, you will have an endless flow of eager apprentice welders. Many won't stay at your center after they complete your bicycle manufacture course, but if you ensure that each course is filled and make your welding positions readily available to course graduates, at least a few are sure to stick around after each course. You can pay apprentice welders minimum wage (by the way, that's about ten times what outsourcing bike companies expect to pay) to allow for mistakes and wasted materials.

After hiring your apprentice welders who have graduated from your course, make sure they can create strong welds, then start them back on welding racks for bikes so mistakes will not be so costly. Even though welding bike racks will be included in your training course, I recommend that you return these graduates to welding bike racks after you've hired them as regular employees. They will have completed welds on bike frame materials during the course and should have completed a bike for their own use before being certified. But you will want to be sure they have mastered this welding process before you allow them to weld frames that will be sold by your organization. Then have them run many welds on scrap frame material for inspection before allowing them to prep and weld actual frames and forks.

By the time they are ready to weld bike frames they will have reached the master welder level and you can give them a raise to something around ten dollars an hour. Keep them around to manufacture your frames long enough for their position to be impressive on their resume, but then help them move on to a higher paying welding job in your community. If your career training system is flowing well, there will be more apprentices ready to seamlessly move into the master welder role. By creating this continuous flow of training to apprentice to master welder, your program will not only create bikes, but new lives for people who may have otherwise never broken free of poverty.

I'm sure I've created far more questions than answers in this introduction to this chapter. I mean, who's crazy enough to manufacture bikes locally? Who's crazy enough to manufacture anything locally? All manufacturing is done by mega corporations in far off countries, right? Don't forget that local manufacture was the only way products were produced just over a hundred years ago. Those of us who live in the most developed countries have lost this entrepreneurial spirit. In fact, countries that are still working to meet some of the developed world's standards are in a far better position to take on bicycle manufacturing simply because they never lost the spirit and pride of manufacturing their own products. If they don't have it, they can often find a way to make it.

Check your area for small manufacturers who work with steel. You might even be lucky enough to find a local bike manufacturer. Get to know them and learn from them. Let their confidence in manufacturing rub off on you.

When I first opened my bike shop, half of my business was welding. I was owner, operator, master mechanic and welder all in one rather overworked package. In fact, the welding side of the business is one reason I named my bike shop Ironclad Bicycles. I had learned every conceivable welding process at our local community college and set up my shop so I could confidently undertake any welding project my customers brought me. From truck trailers to sauna ovens I did it all. That's not to say I never suffered a few flutters of concern as I stared at bizarre line drawings scribbled onto paper napkins (the most common form of "design drawings" I received). But I always found a way to work with my customers and then build them just what they wanted. So remember, even if you are feeling a bit queasy about all of this manufacturing stuff, if I can do it, you and your team can do it.

Next I'll discuss some of the details necessary to successful bicycle manufacture, but realize that a shift into a *can do* mindset regarding manufacture will likely be your most important first step.

Why Steel and Why TIG Welding?

As the bike industry has moved into exotic metals and now even plastic cloth (aka carbon fiber) to manufacture bikes, you might wonder why I only recommend steel for the manufacture of social bikes. Most important is that steel can be easily welded for repairs and modifications. Remember that the bikes you create at your center may never return to a professional mechanic. They will travel deep into inner cities or out to the remotest areas of the world. Their original owner will not be their last. They may be called to duty to transport unimaginable loads. If they are made of steel and they break, anyone with the most basic type of welding equipment will be able to repair them. And this ease of welding will allow future owners to modify racks, add motors or sidecars, or change them into rickshaws, bicycle machines and rolling businesses such as food sales or mobile bicycle repair.

Steel is also the easiest metal to weld. The heat affected zone around the weld is quite large meaning that it distributes heat well and avoids overheating that can cause burn through. Steel's properties also allow it to be welded in the dirtiest conditions. Contaminants simply burn off leaving a strong weld. This ease of welding also means that when a mistake is made it can be cut or ground away and the same steel welded again.

In contrast, aluminum is terribly finicky to weld. The heat affected zone around the weld is very small so even a weld that seems to be going along nicely can suddenly flash and burn a big hole in the surrounding base metal. It also must be absolutely clean or the weld will absorb the impurities and break under the slightest load. Because aluminum is porous, unlike steel, it is like a sponge to oils, dirt and other contaminants. This guarantees that welding used aluminum will result in weak, dangerous welds. In other words, if you were to build your social bikes out of aluminum, they could never be repaired if they broke. They could also never be modified by future owners such as adding racks or turning them into a mobile business vehicle. Also, if a mistake is made during manufacture, the mistake cannot be easily corrected because grinding or cutting the metal is likely to infuse contaminants into the weld area.

Titanium, magnesium and other exotic metals are also a bad choice as they are extremely expensive and difficult to weld.

Carbon fiber and its variations such as bamboo and other unusual materials run into similar concerns of expense and inability to repair or modify. Most importantly, your entire manufacturing set up would be completely different from welding steel, thus removing the potential of expanding into the manufacture of countless other sorts of bikes and bicycle machines (more in the next chapter). While bamboo bikes are becoming popular as a fad item for privileged people, they are only seeing success for developing countries in this export realm. Our local partners tell me that local, struggling people in places where bamboo grows do not want to ride bamboo bikes because bamboo is seen as a poor person's material. Also, keep in mind that the resins used to hold the bamboo together are toxic.

So, back to steel, but now you might ask: Why TIG welding? Spelled out, TIG stands for tungsten inert gas, but "TIG" is the common term. Before I get into what TIG welding is all about and why it is the best for welding social bikes, it's important to know what welding is in general. The simplest explanation is that welding melts the two pieces of base metal together so they actually become one. This distinguishes welding from other ways to join metal such as brazing, which sticks the two pieces together with a lower melting point metal, similar to the way glue functions.

TIG welding is the most expensive welding process because the machine itself is the most expensive. Also, argon, which is the most common shielding gas for TIG welding, is one of the most expensive gases to buy. But TIG welding offers far more control than any other type of welding. It is the most refined arc welding process out of the three; the other two being MIG and stick. Arc welding creates an arc of electricity between the welding torch and the base metal, which melts the metal. The torch that creates the arc in TIG welding is no bigger than a marking pen and the filler metal held in the welder's opposite hand is as delicate as a pencil lead. Heat is regulated by a foot control, much like a sewing machine. The welder can sit comfortably and weld as slowly as necessary to create excellent welds. In fact, anyone who can use a sewing machine has a good chance of being a good TIG welder.

MIG welding, which stands for metal inert gas, is cheap because the machines are cheap and it can use less expensive gases. However, the automatic wire feed mechanism prevents full control, which results in poor quality welds that either move too fast, preventing full penetration, or too slow, cutting into the base metal. Also, the torch is so large and cumbersome that tight welds between bicycle frame tubes are impossible. Most mass merchant bike frames are welded using MIG. Take a closer look at one of these and you will see undercutting, welds sitting on top of the tubes, and disturbing gaps where the torch could not reach.

Shielded metal arc welding, also called stick welding, is the most common arc welding process around the world. The machines are relatively inexpensive, the materials are cheap (no gas needed) and the process can weld massive pieces of steel together. This is the sort of welding used in building construction, mining and farming operations. While a master stick welder can work wonders even with somewhat thin walled steel, the process is too crude to ensure quality welds in the tight corners necessary in bicycle frame building. It is interesting to note, though that most TIG welding machines come with a stick welding set up, so as you expand your welding operation you could take on larger projects that would move faster with stick.

Oxyacetylene welding, braze welding and brazing are a few other ways steel bike frames are commonly built, but I don't recommend them for social bikes for several reasons. This process uses a gas torch to melt the metal, usually a mix of oxygen and acetylene, thus the term oxyacetylene welding. While the oxyacetylene welding process is inexpensive, it is difficult to master and very prone to mistakes. Braze welding and fillet brazing have similar pitfalls.

Brazing with lugs has resulted in gorgeous bike frames because this process relies on carefully crafted lugs, which the frame tubes fit into before they're brazed together with silver or brass. These lugs can be artfully crafted with ornate designs, which is why you will see very expensive bikes built this way. But each lug must be created with specific angles and openings for each junction and each size of bike. Using such a rigid process to manufacture social bikes would eliminate all expansion opportunities for other types of bikes, machines, trailers and accessories.

Oxyacetylene welding, braze welding and brazing are also not commonly used in other industries besides plumbing and jewelry making so your trainees would not benefit from career development as much as they would by learning TIG welding.

It wouldn't hurt to have a set of oxyacetylene tanks and torches at your center just to show your trainees the difference. Oxyacetylene can also be handy for cutting large pieces of steel when there is no electricity nearby. This might come in handy if you expand into large welding jobs.

I realize that in some parts of the world, argon is so expensive that TIG welding becomes almost impossible. One cumbersome but effective method of dealing with this is to build a transparent welding box around each of your frame building jigs that will hold and recycle the argon rather than spilling it out into the room. Such a box would have welding gloves attached much like an incubator and a sealed lid and entry for the torch cable. This might sound strange, but such welding boxes are actually fairly common because titanium frame building requires them.

For an excellent overview of welding types, shop set up and safety visit: www.gowelding.org. The website is a bit littered with outside advertisers, but if you can ignore them and focus on the main body of the site you will find lots of useful information.

Manufacturing Training Methods

Your clients who sign up for your manufacturing training module are going to be a unique bunch. These are the craftsmen and craftswomen who already love to make things. Some will be easy to spot with handcrafted add-ons to their bikes or you might hear them talk with pride about a clever way they repaired a friend's refrigerator by fabricating a new part out of junk. These may be your future manufacturing specialists. Don't let them leave your center without telling them about your next social bike manufacturing course.

As I mentioned in Chapter 8, this course must be hands on. You will include some classroom time to discuss social bike design concepts, the principles of your program, welding concepts and safety, metal preparation prior to welding, and metallurgy, but the training will not begin until they actually strike a spark with a welding torch.

All novice welders have to run a lot of welds before their hand, eye and foot coordination settles into a groove. Find a source for new, inexpensive flat steel, cut it into small sections and have your students run weld after weld until they can consistently create perfect welds. If you are not a master welder, you'll have to hire one in the beginning at least for weld inspections. As your training course progresses, your master frame welders can fill this role.

As you can imagine, handling a class of five or ten manufacturing students in this section of the course will be tough. You will need multiple welding machines and stations, or will have to stagger their practice sessions so only a few practice at once. If this is possible, great. Keep them at your center so you or your trainers can supervise their training. Another option is to partner with a local vocational school or community college that offers a welding course. Even if this school does not offer TIG welding or requires students to start with oxyacetylene or stick welding, this practice will transfer to TIG. But they should skip MIG. MIG welding is all about setting up the machine and does not require the skill and coordination of TIG.

Once your students can run perfect welds with TIG on flat steel, have them begin practicing on pipe steel. If your local vocational school offers a pipe welding course, definitely include it in your partnership. Bicycle frame welding is pipe welding and pipe welding requires additional skill to keep the proper torch and filler metal angles that result in perfect welds around the entire pipe.

Once your students have mastered pipe welding, they are ready to start melting some steel for your program. Have them start by welding the racks for your social bikes. Many of the social bikes designed by our local partners include integrated front and rear racks. These racks must first be fabricated out of small tube steel before they are welded to the bikes. You can also design some of these racks to be sold separately for customer bikes or added to bikes you refurbish. You can purchase this rack steel in long sections at a bulk cost so if a student makes a mistake, there will be minimal loss. The sales of these student-built racks will help cover the costs of the training.

Some students won't get this far in the course. Others will graduate and get hired at your center, but won't move past the apprentice welder level of welding your racks before they move on to something else. Only the most passionate and talented students you hire will be fit for promotion to the next, master welding level where they actually weld your social bike frames and forks.

Setting up Your Manufacturing Workshop
Just as with every aspect of your Social Bike Business program, start the set up of your manufacturing workshop to fit your budget. If this means just one welding machine and frame building station, that's okay. Don't be tempted to invest money you don't have in more or fancier equipment than you need to get started. As your program grows and bike sales bring in profits, you can invest those profits in more and improved welding stations.

If you or the others on your leadership team do not have much welding experience, I recommend hiring a local welder to help you design the floor plan of your workshop. You will be surprised at the many important details necessary to ensure future manufacturing can move smoothly. For instance, each TIG welding machine should be hardwired in place by an experienced electrician for safety. Hardwiring is not required, but it will prevent potentially dangerous mishaps with a cord that is simply plugged into a wall socket. Hardwiring your machines will make them very difficult to move later, so be sure you know where you want them and allow plenty of room for your welders to work.

Welding machines use a much larger gauge of electrical wire than other electrical devices. Have your electrician set up separate circuit breakers for each welding machine. These circuit breakers, just like the wires, must handle a much larger electrical load than other devices. To give you an idea, in the U.S., a welding machine requires a 220 volt and a minimum 50 amp supply while our regular household or shop machines only require 120 volts and 15 amps. Even if your country normally uses 220 volt electricity, the amps will likely not suffice so you will still need a separate, beefier circuit breaker to handle each machine. Without this separate set up, the wires supplying your machines will overheat and burst into flames, so skimping on this is not at all worth it and likely not even legal.

TIP: Imagine how people will move around your manufacturing area before you design it.

Consider where your steel will be stored, how your welders will access it, where cutting, mitering and other preparation processes will take place and how much room they will need. When you choose the final place for each of your welding machines these welding stations must have ample room around them to allow your welders to work without running into other people or equipment.

Another very important consideration is that each of your welders must be covered from head to toe to protect them from radiation burns. Any skin that is exposed within the vicinity of where welding is taking place will suffer the worst sunburn within seconds. Prolonged exposure can be very dangerous. Have your welders wear either leather, cotton or other natural fabrics because these materials do not catch fire easily. Never allow any of your welders to wear synthetic clothing because it is combustible. Their hair should be covered by a cotton or other natural fabric welding cap and they must wear a high quality welding helmet with the highest level of protective lens.

This important safety concern applies to the set up of your workshop because anyone in the vicinity when welding is underway must also be covered in the same manner. Therefore, your manufacturing workshop must not be in the path of any common destination within your center. For instance, it must not be between your welcome area and the bathrooms or along a direct passage to the only side or back door. Everyone in the welding area must be trained to cover themselves when welding is underway or move away from the welding stations.

Besides your welding machines, each welding station will need its own welding table and frame building jig. A welding table is simply a table made out of steel so it will conduct electricity. Each TIG welding machine will have a ground cable that attaches to the table or jig to allow the welding current to make a full circle, otherwise known as a circuit. This is what enables the electrical arc at the torch for welding. Build each welding table slightly higher than regular table height to allow your welders to sit on a stool and not have to stoop when standing.

Frame building jigs are essential to building straight frames that meet your design specifications. They are basically a rack and clamp system that holds each frame tube absolutely still as the welder welds them together. When two pieces of base metal are welded together, the weld actually pulls them together, which distorts the placement of the tubes. Without a jig, your bicycle frames would come out looking like twisted modern art with little resemblance to a bicycle.

Bicycle frame building jigs can be extremely sophisticated and expensive purchased from a frame building supplier, or as basic as a backyard project made of scrap wood. At the start, I recommend going at least a bit fancier than the scrap wood concept because wooden jigs only last for a few frames before they are completely warped and ruined. Check your area for bicycle frame builders who can help you build your jigs. Frame building has become a popular hobby in recent years as more classes are offered and bicycle enthusiasts try their hand at building gorgeous frames. Most of these frame builders use lugs and brazing, but the jig set up is virtually the same. You can also check online for countless jig designs offered by such hobbyists. The key factors you will want to aim for with your jigs are:

- Durability – can withstand the heat from welding many frames.
- Weld accessibility – your welders should be able to weld entirely around the tubes without adjusting the jig.
- Adjustability – the jig should be adjustable for different frame sizes including extra small (smallest adults and teenagers), small, medium, large and extra large (largest adults).
- Clamp quality – the jig must hold the frame tubes perfectly still.

Just as important as your jigs will be your mitering set up. Mitering is the process of cutting the frame tubes at a rounded angle so they join together without leaving gaps at the designed angle. Even the smallest gap can cause a weak weld that will result in frame failure. While many bicycle frame builder hobbyists will cut their miter joints by hand using a hacksaw and file, for faster production you will need to use a hole saw in a drill press. Just one of these mitering set ups will service your workshop even if you have several welding stations, because your welders will generally be at different stages of the frame building process.

Also set up a separate metal cutting area. While custom-made bicycle frame tubing sets are available from Asian factories, you will likely find that buying your frame tubing in bulk from a local supplier will be more affordable, offer better career training to your students and allow more versatility for your manufacturing. I only recommend using high quality chromoly steel rather than the lower grade basic carbon steel, so make sure your supplier carries chromoly before you order. With lengths of bulk steel tubing your welders will have to make an initial cut before mitering the tubes to their exact lengths and shapes. A chop saw with a clamp and metal cutting blade can work well. Handheld pipe cutters can also work, but they take more time and are more difficult to control.

You will also need to set up a bench vise, minimum four inches wide, where your welders can clamp tubes to refine cuts, file off burs, grind off mistakes, and shape metal for other projects.

A tube bender, also called a pipe bender, will be necessary for bending the small tubing used to build your racks. An inexpensive handheld or vise-held bender sold at any plumbing supply store should do the trick.

Handheld power tools such as a grinder, drill, and Dremel tool will be helpful for finishing frames. You will also need full sets of files, thread cutting dies and facing tools with fittings that are standard to bicycle frame building.

You will need a frame alignment and finishing area. Your jigs should produce close to perfect frames with the rear triangle aligned with the front triangle, the dropouts parallel, the bottom bracket shell perpendicular, and so on. But chances are that each frame is going to need a shove or two for perfect alignment.

The simplest alignment tool is a piece of string tied to one dropout, stretched around the head tube and then tied to the other dropout. Use a ruler or measuring tape to measure the distance between the string and the seat tube on each side. These two distances must match perfectly or the rear wheel will go in a different direction than the front—not a good idea. If the distances are extremely off, the frame needs to be scrapped. If the distances are only slightly different you simply need to adjust the frame by hand. Steel is so easy to work with you can likely make the adjustment with two people. Secure a rear wheel in the dropouts to prevent them being smashed together. Lay the front triangle on a raised platform with one person standing on it and have the other person press gently down at the dropouts. Check the alignment after each press and make sure not to press too hard because there is the danger of moving past alignment. Even though steel can handle adjustments better than most other metals, if you have to adjust the frame back and forth too many times you will weaken the steel.

Facing tools are expensive but very important for finishing frames.

Even though your bottom brackets and head tubes are perfectly aligned, they will still have small imperfections. Facing tools made for finishing bottom bracket shells and head tubes shave off these imperfections so that the bottom brackets and headsets you install will be perfectly aligned. Without facing, the bottom bracket and headset bearings will suffer uneven loads and constantly wear out.

Brake bosses will also have to be perfectly aligned to ensure the brake pads meet the rims. If brake bosses are welded wrong, they must be ground off and rewelded. This is risky because the welder could easily grind too far and ruin the frame. Set up brake boss alignment systems as part of your jigs to save your welders time aligning them and to avoid this problem.

A ventilation system will be necessary for the health and safety of your workers, not only for each welding station, but for your paint booth as well. Any heating and cooling professional can set up a simple system that will do the trick. Make sure vents sit directly above each welding area and the paint booth and that the fan has enough power to draw welding and paint fumes away from the workers. Fumes from welding new steel are not very harmful, but any welds done on used, painted metal, perhaps for repairs or modifications, can be very toxic as the paint turns to fumes. So it's best to set up an effective ventilation system from the start.

Your paint booth needs to be completely enclosed to keep out dust and other particles that could settle into the new paint. It will need an adjustable stand or hanging mechanism that holds the completed frames, forks and racks at about eye level to allow the painter to spray straight onto each tube. The stand must not clamp the item anywhere it needs to be painted. Painting complex items with many angles such as bike frames and racks takes a lot of practice because overspray always lands on the tubes behind and can leave a dull surface. Investing in high quality paint and painting equipment, including a professional air compressor and paint gun, will greatly improve your painters' results. Along with the paint booth equipment, you will also need to supply coveralls and high quality, protective masks for your painters to use inside the paint booth. Even with a good ventilation system, fumes will swirl around the painter so this mask will complete the protection from the fumes. Check for local regulations.

Safety systems will become second nature to you and your welders after some practice. But all of you will have to remain vigilant for the safety of trainees and people who wander into the welding area.

Personal safety centers around covering skin with leather or cotton clothing as well as a high quality welding helmet for each welder. The clothing can be quite thin so welders don't have to overheat in warm weather. Another benefit of TIG welding in this regard is that the welders' gloves can also be quite thin and fit them well. This allows for better control of the torch. In contrast, stick and oxyacetylene welding throw off so much heat and cause so much metal spatter that very thick leather bibs and gloves are required.

For safety around the welding and preparation equipment, start by making sure that all users are fully familiar with the safety requirements for each. These can be found in the manuals that accompany each machine. Keep these manuals in an obvious place for quick reference and show all your welders where they are. Have plenty of safety glasses and ear protectors near machines metal preparation machines.

Remove all flammable or combustible items from the area around each of your welding stations. This includes all paper, solvents, cleaning supplies, paint, rags and sawdust. Keep a fire extinguisher nearby in case a combustible item does end up near a welder. Countless sparks of tiny burning metal fragments fly during welding and just one of these burning fragments can start a fire in a forgotten cardboard box or in the corner of an unswept floor. Sparks also fly during grinding and cutting metal. So keep your welding, grinding and cutting areas as clean as possible by scheduling a daily cleanup that includes sweeping and removing all combustibles, no matter how small they are.

Designing Social Bikes

Before reading on, make sure that you are familiar with the terminology used to describe the different parts of a bike frame. You'll find a diagram in Appendix A of this book.

I've described the general features of a social bike throughout this book—affordable, durable, built for transportation and carrying loads—but there are many potential variations once you begin designing your organization's social bikes to be built at your center. First, and as always when starting a new element of your program, find out what the struggling people in your area need. Ask them what sort of trips they would make with a bicycle. Will they travel long distances or is there a bus or train service they can take their bikes on? Is the terrain flat with well maintained roads or hilly with lots of potholes? These details will help you and your team narrow down the design choices. For instance:

- Flat terrain with good roads and long travel distance might point to single speed bikes with 27 or 28 inch wheels and narrow, smooth tires.
- Hilly terrain with dirt roads and lots of pot holes will need gears and likely 26 inch mountain bike wheels with fat knobby tires.
- If there is a bus or train service that takes bikes, this will limit how long the wheelbase can be.
- If your area has a lot of rain, fenders will be necessary.
- And all social bikes must come with at least one rack, preferably in the back because loads upfront affect the bike's steering, which limits a front rack's carrying capacity. Both rear and front racks are ideal.

The type of bike you and your team choose will determine the frame angles and tube lengths of the bikes you produce. The wheel size you choose will help determine the needed length of the stays and fork blades and will designate the placement of your brake bosses. The choice of a narrow tire would allow a narrower opening between fork blades and avoid the need to bend the chain stays to accommodate a wide tire, but keep in mind that a wide tire could never be used on the bike.

Some angles are extremely important to the resulting performance of the bike. For instance, a steep head tube angle (closer to vertical) will make the bike more responsive, but less stable, and give a harsher ride. You will see steep head tubes on special purpose racing bikes. A head tube angle that's not so steep will add stability and absorb more shock, but will be less responsive. These are not massive changes in angle. Head tube angles should range between 70 and 75 degrees. Outside that range, the bike will behave strangely and could be difficult to control. When considering the head tube angle of your bikes, you will also have to take into account the amount of rake you design into your forks. Rake is the curving sweep or angle of a fork that sets the front wheel hub off from the main line of the head tube. No rake causes a jarring ride. Too much rake and the rider will have to force the wheel to turn.

The seat tube angle is less important, though you will want the rider to be positioned above the pedal line to ensure he or she can achieve maximum power from their legs. The seat tube angle must be less than ninety degrees in order to absorb shock, but angling it too far will diminish handling and waste the pedal energy of the rider.

Tube sizing choices will also be important. You'll need to stick with good quality chromoly steel, so find out what sizes your local dealer can provide. For the main frame (head tube, down tube, seat tube and top tube), one and an eighth inch tube diameter with a .049 inch wall thickness will do a nice job. This is a large enough diameter for stiffness and strength without going overboard. If you have to go with a smaller diameter, be sure to increase the wall thickness to reach a similar strength. For your stays, one inch tube diameter with the .049 inch wall thickness

will work well.

Perhaps the most important choice of tube size will be your seat tube because it must match the most common seat post size found in your area. For instance, a tube with a one and an eighth inch outside diameter and a .049 inch wall thickness will match a 26.8 inch seat post. If this size seat post is commonly available in your area, or you believe your center can do a good job of supplying your area with this size of seat post through your vendors, this will work fine. Otherwise you will need to change either the tube diameter or wall thickness to match a more common seat post size. And since you will want to buy your tubing in bulk, you will likely need to change your top tube and down tube sizes to match.

Bottom bracket height is another design decision you and your team will have to make. If your social bikes will be used in rough terrain, a higher bottom bracket will assist with clearance over rocks, city curbs and other obstacles. Take a look at the difference in bottom bracket heights on a road bike and a mountain bike. Mountain bikes will always have a higher bottom bracket in order to clear rocks. But the higher the bottom bracket, the higher the rider and this can throw off balance and control.

Regardless of these finer design details, stick to the common "diamond frame" design that has proven its strength and durability for more than a century. This is the most common frame design. The diagram in the Appendix section is a diamond framed bike. I recommend starting with what used to be called a "men's" frame design as shown in the diagram. They are stronger than the step through, dropped top tube design originally made to allow the rider to wear a dress. This picture shows an example of one. By dropping the top tube you lose the strength of the triangle, the strongest geometrical shape of all. As a bike messenger, I broke several step through framed bikes and at my bike shop, encountered countless broken step through frame bikes. They generally snap at the top tube where it meets the seat tube, which suggests the lost triangular strength. Once your bicycle production is going full steam, you can consider experimenting with step through frame bikes.

You will also have to plan for five frame sizes: extra small (for the smallest adults and teenagers), small, medium, large, and extra large (for the largest adults). Top tube, down tube and seat stay angles and length will change. Seat tube and head tube length will change. But the head tube angle, seat tube angle and chain stays will not change. Each of these different sizes will result in the same feel and ride for the rider that fits the bike. As I mentioned above, you will want to use a frame jig type that can be easily adjusted to different sizes.

Some of the tricky bits you'll have to work out with your team include how to attach the rear dropouts and how to attach the seat stays to the seat tube. The chromoly steel pipe you order for your stays will need to be mitered, cut and/or crimped depending on the design you choose. Study different designs on various bikes.

Regarding rear dropouts, at first you will have to purchase these from a wholesale vendor. Later you might add forging, stamping or CNC machines to your shop that could produce your own dropout designs. Make sure that the dropouts you choose have an angled, horizontal slot that is at least one and an eighth inches long. The angle keeps the rim aligned with the brakes in all positions. The long slot will allow even a bike that originally had gears to accommodate a one speed coaster brake wheel, which needs room for chain tension adjustment. Remember that many of your social bikes will never return to your center or any bike shop for repairs. If the original rear wheel breaks or the gears or brakes stop working for any reason, a coaster brake wheel could be installed and the bike brought back to life. The more options you allow for the repair of your bikes the better.

There's a similar choice for forks. Many of your wholesale vendors will stock affordable, good quality chromoly forks with the steering tube already threaded and the blades already painted; in all the sizes to fit your five frame sizes. Eventually, your welders should have no problem producing excellent quality forks, but purchasing your first forks from your vendors will help you focus on refining your frame building system.

This brings up another design decision: whether to go with a threaded or threadless headset system. Until about 15 years ago, there was no choice, which made things much easier. Threaded headsets have been around since the earliest diamond frame bikes. These require a threaded fork for the headset to thread onto and a quill stem that inserts inside the fork's steering tube. But some mountain bike designers decided that attaching the stem to the outside of the steering tube would save a few grams of weight. This threadless design may be a bit stronger, too, but threaded steering systems generally don't fail so this is not a concern. Because threaded headsets and forks have been around so much longer than threadless, you will likely want to choose threaded to give the most replacement options from the used parts available. Another advantage of threaded headsets is that most people are familiar with how they work. They know that if they loosen the bolt at the top of the stem, they can raise or lower the stem. But if someone loosens the bolts that hold a threadless stem in place and raise the stem, this loosens the entire headset, which can cause the rider to crash. Even so, check your area. There's a slight chance that it has been flooded with bikes using the threadless system, which might make it the better choice.

Your vendors might also carry ready-made bottom bracket shells. Otherwise your bottom bracket shells will have to be threaded to match the most common bottom bracket thread count, so compare the cost of manufacturing them at your center with purchasing the shells from a vendor.

Rather than trying to reinvent the bicycle, the easiest way for you and your team to start designing your social bikes is to find a bike that is close to what you need to produce. Copy the angles of that bike and create a prototype to discover what would be involved in manufacturing that type of bike. Then add the racks, parts, wheels and perhaps fenders that are part of your design needs and look for concerns. After you've succeeded in building the prototype based on an existing bike, you can begin careful, incremental modifications to improve the design to better fit the needs of the people you plan to serve with these bikes.

The danger in the design process is that we are all prone to wander off into fantasy designs. Even if you can stay focused, all of the others on your team will also be tempted by such distractions. Listen for buzz terms like "innovation" and "no one has ever tried *this* before" because they can lead all of you right into the crazy maze that has engulfed our entire bike industry. The more farfetched the design, the more expensive and less durable it will be, including the likely inability to repair it once it is broken. In other words, you will be designing bikes for rich people who can throw things away when they break and then buy the next farfetched, newfangled bike. One positive outcome of such a detour, providing that all of you manage to retrace your steps back to designing social bikes for regular folks, is that you will gain empathy for the influencers in the bike industry. They haven't abandoned basic bike designs because they're evil and hate poor people. They're just completely distracted by crazy, "innovative" designs and profits.

Keep in mind that the problem is *not* a lack of innovation. The bike industry is dripping with innovation. The problem is a lack of basic, durable, affordable and easy-to-repair bikes for everyone else.

There are several bicycle frame building books available, but most are too specific to hobby frame builders to be much use to you. Here are a few I would recommend because they go into greater detail about design concepts than most:

- *The Paterek Manual for Bicycle Framebuilders*, by Tim Paterek
- *The Proteus Framebuilding Book: A Guide for the Novice Bicycle Framebuilder*, by Dr. Paul Proteus

To learn why the tiniest changes in design can dramatically affect a bicycle's durability and handling, read *Bicycling Science*, by David Gordon Wilson. It goes into far more detail than you will need, but it clearly shows that bicycles are not simple machines. It will be a good reference book for your center's bookshelf.

Before moving on, I have to make sure you include two more very important details in your design process: color of paint and design of your decals. These can be a lot of fun to work out. You'll want to start with just one paint color to keep costs down. Again, work with your neighborhood residents to learn what color they prefer. You won't get a full consensus, but you'll certainly learn which colors to avoid and which colors would be popular. Then your team can make the final choice. For the decals, you can get as creative as you like, maybe even open the design up to a contest. Work with a local decal or sticker maker that produces quality products. You can name your bikes something that will resonate with your locals and include your organization's name and logo. After applying the decals, likely to the head tube and down tube, cover the whole frame with a final clear coat to protect them.

Choosing Parts & Assembling

Spec'ing your bikes, that is, choosing the parts that will go onto the bikes you build, can also be a lot of fun. Once your frame manufacturing is underway, you will need to seek out a different type of wholesale vendor that specializes in supplying parts to original equipment manufacturers (OEM) like your organization. You will set up an OEM account with each of them, which will price the packages of parts they sell for your bikes lower than the wholesale prices you would pay from your other vendors.

After designing your bikes, you will already know some of the spec choices you'll have to make, for instance: wheel size, gears or no gears, seat post diameter, quill or threadless stem, fenders or no fenders, and so on. You'll also be familiar with the used parts that are most easily found in your area, which should influence your choices to increase your bikes' reparability. Here are some recommendations on further details to help you spec your bikes for disadvantaged people:

- Choose aluminum rims, double walled if possible, not only because they are usually stronger than steel (really cheap aluminum rims aren't, so be careful), but because they do not rust. Also, in rainy climates, the brake pads will grab aluminum when steel rims would mean no brakes at all.
- Choose the heaviest duty solid axles available, chromoly if possible. Make sure that the front and rear axles are the same diameter and both use fifteen millimeter nuts, never quick release skewers.
- Do not spec *any* quick release skewers on your bikes! Not on your wheels or your seat binders. Quick releases were developed for racers who are trying to save seconds during a race. Somehow the bike industry forgot the other benefactors of this "innovative" design: thieves. Don't make it easy on them! Also, very few people know how to use a quick release properly, which is why they are the cause of far too many serious crashes when wheels fall off.
- Spec as few bolt and nut sizes as possible. Your wheels will be

held on with a fifteen millimeter nut. A common seat post binder nut is fourteen millimeters as is the most common crank nut. If you can choose a quill stem with a fourteen millimeter bolt, you could supply a 14/15 millimeter wrench with each bike you sell and give your bike buyers the ability to repair and adjust their new bike themselves.

- Avoid internal gear hubs. They are far too expensive and cannot be repaired easily.

- Spec only rear gears if possible. This will cut down on costs dramatically because you will eliminate the front derailleur and a shift lever and cut the cost of your crankset. At your price range this will mean eight gears or fewer and that might be plenty.

- Spec the simplest most durable shift levers you can find. Avoid plastic shift levers, including grip shifting style, because they do not hold up to heavy use. I realize that simple, durable shift levers made of metal are getting very difficult to find, which is why One Street has begun the process of manufacturing them ourselves. Read more on this later in this chapter.

- The shift levers and brake levers you spec will likely come with regular steel cables. Consider changing out at least the shift cables to stainless steel cables to prevent corrosion. Brake levers provide more force to the cable, so corrosion isn't as much of an issue, but if you can also switch them to stainless, that would be ideal.

- Spec a three piece crank and bottom bracket. Do not even consider a one piece crank. A one piece crank and bottom bracket will be much cheaper, but also much less durable than a three piece crank.

- Spec the heaviest duty chain you can find. Oddly, it will likely be the cheapest, because bike industry priorities—lightweight, fragile, not repairable—are the inverse of Social Bike Business priorities. Hopefully your OEM vendors still stock the old style, heavy, clunky chains that can still be broken and reassembled many times without being compromised. More expensive chains cannot be broken with a chain tool or hammer and nail, the most common "chain tool" in remote areas of the world. Note that chains for one speed bikes and geared bikes are very different and not interchangeable, so make sure to order what you need.

- Do not skimp on seat post length! You might sell a medium sized bike to someone it fits perfectly, but social bikes will last for generations and future owners might not fit perfectly. Spec the longest seat post available and you will increase your bike's versatility for many sizes of riders.

One more decision you and your team will have to make is whether to spec a freewheel or a freehub on your bikes. Freewheels are more common in many parts of the world. They are also easy to replace if they break without the entire wheel having to be replaced. But freehubs support the rear axle better, making the axles less prone to bending. Also, if the teeth of the gears wear down or break, only the gears have to be replaced, not the whole ratcheting unit. However, freehub gears are generally about the same price as a whole freewheel. All of these considerations make this decision less clear than the others I listed above. Factor in cost, which one is more common in your area, and replaceability versus axle protection.

Another not so clear choice will be crank arm length. The longer the arm, the more torque the rider will have on the down stroke, but longer crank arms provide less clearance. Short arms offer more control when quick adjustments are necessary such as in traffic and give more clearance to the ground and the front tire, but lose torque. Again, check for the most common crank arm length in your area. In the U.S., 170mm is the most common found on mountain bikes, but 175mm is also common. Both are a happy medium between sizes that are considered unusually long and unusually short, so would be a good start if you are otherwise unsure.

One recommendation you might consider is to attend the closest bicycle trade show to your area. In Europe, the trade show is called Eurobike www.eurobike-show.com. In the U.S., the trade show is called Interbike www.interbike.com. At a trade show you can meet with your vendors in person and actually touch the parts and accessories you're considering buying from them.

While assembling your bikes, take special care to ensure all the parts will last as long as possible. For instance: the headset cups will have to be pressed in to align perfectly; all bearing units, including the hubs will have to be well greased with quality bicycle-grade grease; chains will have to have factory grease removed and be re-lubed with a quality light oil; and new cables will have to be pre-stretched. Work with your master mechanic to create a system and checklist for your assemblers to follow. In Appendix C you'll find an overhaul checklist that will offer ideas on the details to include.

Insurance & Manufacturing Requirements

To add sufficient insurance that covers damages or injuries caused by manufacturing defects in your bikes, check with your insurance provider. Just as with your other insurance plans, buy enough coverage, but no more than necessary. If you can find an insurance company that is familiar with bicycle manufacturing, that will be ideal.

Both your government and your insurance provider will require you to meet the bicycle frame and fork manufacturing standards that have been set for your country. Find them through your government or your vendors. You will be shocked at how simple it is to meet the required standards. In fact, because quality and safety are priorities to you, I'm quite sure you will have anticipated meeting such standards anyway.

The quality of the frames, forks and racks welded at your center will have to be tested to prove that you are meeting the required standards. The easiest way will be to contract with a product test center in your area. This will only have to be done very infrequently with just a few sample frames, forks and racks from your manufacturing line. Check your country's requirements for testing frequency.

In the U.S., the Consumer Product Safety Commission (CPSC) sets the standards for bicycles. You can search for the requirements from their home page at www.cpsc.gov using "requirements for bicycles 16 CFR part 1512." Sometimes only a summary document comes up. Find all the sections of the law. If you can't find all of them from a search, you might have to contact someone at the CPSC.

Manufacturing Parts

Once you and your team are comfortable welding frames, forks and racks at your center, you will likely want to add other products to manufacture. In the next chapter, I'll discuss adding different types of bikes, bicycle machines and trailers to your manufacturing line up. But manufacturing bike parts might become necessary before you move into this larger item production.

As I noted above, One Street added a components manufacturing program to our lineup in 2011 because we found that basic shift levers were no longer available in most places around the world and other basic parts were becoming hard to find such as affordable durable rear derailleurs and heavy duty chains.

One Street Components operates just like any other One Street program by working with our local partners to produce the bike parts we design. In 2013, our shift levers will be ready for production with more part designs underway. The shift levers will use a simple aluminum casting process and assembly with common parts. The local partners we work with will have to follow our design guidelines, but they will sell the shifters they make and keep the profits to invest in their Social Bike Business program. Let us know if you'd like to add this to your manufacturing system.

Whether you take part in One Street Components production or not, keep this manufacturing concept in mind: if you can't find a necessary part, perhaps you can make it.

I realize this chapter has been a very quick overview of many complex considerations, but if you take each step carefully and keep moving forward in your manufacturing set up, you will end up with beautiful new bikes rolling out of your center in the hands of people who truly need them. These clients and customers will have the opportunity to meet the very person who welded their bike frame. And these welders will take pride in knowing the bikes they built are helping their neighbors reach jobs and carry loads they never could have without their bike.

This "new" (actually the original) model of local manufacturing holds the potential of inspiring other industries as these neighborhoods finally pull out of poverty in part because of the beautiful bikes your staff manufactured for their neighbors. Bringing the manufacturing process back down to the local level will build the economies in each community that embraces this model, whether just with bikes or many other products.

Creative Income
Generators &
Program Elements

've placed this chapter last to emphasize that creative additions to your program should never come before your basic services of providing quality, affordable transportation bikes and career training to disadvantaged people. Still, with a thriving bicycle community center and lots of creative people involved, you will find many opportunities to build on these basic services. Consider creative ideas along with the rest of this program expansion section of this book—like optional additions that will only be beneficial if your program is ready for them.

Many of these creative additions will be in the form of products you can manufacture once your bicycle manufacturing system is well established. I'll start with examples of these, including cargo bikes, trailers, rolling businesses and bike machines. You might also attract artists who can help develop crafts to manufacture and sell at your center or expand into public art. The entrepreneurs on your team might be eager to help add business opportunities such as bike rentals or contracting with your local government on bike services in other parts of the community. The bike education services already offered by your staff will also provide the opportunity to expand into regular bike riding and safety skills classes at your center and perhaps even at schools around your community. And of course I can't write a whole book without encouraging some sort of bicycle advocacy. There are very few communities in this world that truly inspire people to choose bicycling as their favorite means of transportation. Those that do, face constant threats from powerful companies who profit when road space and city land is used to move and park motorized vehicles. Every community needs a strong bicycle advocacy movement even to make the slightest progress toward improving conditions for bicycling. I'll cap this chapter off with a few ideas for making your center the hub of bicycle advocacy in your community.

Modified Bikes, Trailers, and Bike Machines

If you do internet searches for cargo bike, mobile bike business, utility cycling, and bicycle vendor you will find a lifetime's worth of inspiration for modified bikes you and your team can build at your center. Again the danger is to wander away from your mission of serving disadvantaged people. Some of the Dutch and Danish cargo bikes sell for over three thousand dollars. Much of this cost is in the fancy parts and paint, but there is also a lot of time and engineering that has to go into the design to ensure these bikes can carry massive loads. Unlike the diamond frame bicycle, these bikes do not have the benefit of more than a century of strength testing. But don't let that stop you from giving this a try once you have the time and resources to spare. Study several designs of cargo bikes and bikes used for mobile businesses. You will also find design concepts and discussions on the internet.

While cargo bikes will come in handy simply for carrying loads and children, the most exciting potential for building modified load carrying bikes is that they could become rolling businesses for graduates of some of your career training modules. For instance, a graduate of both of your bicycle repair modules and your business management module would have all the training they'd need to open their own mobile bicycle repair shop. Any graduate of your business management and sales and customer service modules would be eligible for a rolling business that sold trinkets or snacks to tourists.

Once you begin playing around with modifying bicycles you will be on track to create bikes for disabled people, too. Someone who can't walk could ride a three-wheeled bike with the pedals moved up to a hand pedaling position. Someone with one leg could pedal a bike with an elliptical chainring that propels the bike on a single down stroke. Someone with balance problems could handle a bike with outrigger wheels added. Let your imagination fly as you work with the individuals to create a bike that will work for them.

Bicycle trailers also offer inspiring potential. A rolling business could be attached to a trailer, allowing the owner to detach the bike and use it normally. Bicycle trailers have also proven to be very effective ambulances in remote areas.

However bicycle trailers are surprisingly complex, so do your homework before delving into this manufacturing adventure. Designed poorly they will pull back against the rider or worse, flip over causing a severe crash. They can also swing sideways into the rider or sway violently back and forth. Before embarking on bicycle trailer building, find several different designs on the internet and in your community. Test recommended trailers and study their designs. How do they ensure the load is balanced over the trailer's wheels? Where and how do they attach to the bike? How long are they? How much clearance do they give to the bike's rear tire? Trailers that attach near the rear axle are supposed to offer the greatest stability, but the attachment mechanism is far more complex than simply attaching them at the seat post. These details must be worked out carefully in your organization's trailer design before a welding torch comes anywhere near it. Then create a prototype and test it in all extreme situations—massive loads, high speed, cornering, bumpy roads, hill climbing. Make adjustments until all dangerous behaviors are remedied before going into production.

Bike machines are another fanciful addition to your manufacturing lineup. Bicycles can power knife sharpeners, corn grinders, electrical generators, battery chargers, washing machines, water pumps and water filters. The opportunities are endless. Each could become a mobile business for your training graduates or remain at your center for its use or to rent for specific amounts of time. Search the internet for "bicycle powered" and you'll find ideas you never could have imagined. Some operate as bicycles to carry their owners to a place where they can set up shop. Then, with just a few turns of a wrench, the pedals become the power that turns the knife sharpening wheel, grinder, battery charger or other contraption. Before moving into producing many of the same type of machine, ask whether that particular bicycle powered machine is the most needed and in demand.

For instance, a remote rural area might benefit enormously from rentable bicycle powered corn grinders. If your center is in a remote area that has sketchy electrical service, your program itself might benefit from setting up several bicycle powered electrical generators that could provide direct power or charge car batteries to store the

electricity for backup. Your volunteers and even kids in the area will enjoy pedaling a few rounds to build up the juice. Bicycle powered water pumps and filters could also directly benefit your center if your water supply is distant and not trustworthy.

If you and your team want to go into production of bicycle machines to sell, you'll need to narrow your choices or end up wasting an enormous amount of time producing a machine that no one will be interested in. Make sure the machines you produce and sell offer a significant benefit to many people in your area and will be in high demand. Otherwise, keep your bicycle machine creations in the realm of off-duty time for your welders who want to play around.

Crafts and Public Art

As your bicycle refurbishing and repair service builds momentum you'll begin to notice an increasing flow of broken bike parts. I mentioned earlier that scrap metal companies will often pay a good price for loads of steel and aluminum. But crafts and public art could be another way for your center to generate income from these otherwise useless bike pieces.

If you have artists and designers on your team, possibly even volunteers or regular visitors to your center, you could set them to work creating jewelry and crafts from small bike parts. I've seen gorgeous necklaces, earrings and bracelets made from chain pieces, gears, spoke nipples and derailleur pulleys. Tire and tube rubber can be transformed into belts, dog collars, purses and seats. Wheels and frames can be welded into chairs, benches and even bike parking racks. Search the internet for "bicycle art" and "recycled bicycle jewelry" and your imagination will be transported to wondrous new places.

All of these crafts could be sold at your center to generate income. If you hold an annual fundraising event, the most elaborate creations could be auctioned to generate even more funding. You could also leverage the fun of this creativity by holding regular craft making events where people can volunteer their time to make these bike parts crafts to help generate income for your programs. You might also live in an area that attracts lots of tourists in which case you won't want to limit your craft materials to bike parts. Local basket making, carving and other skills can be tapped to support your center.

If your area does enjoy such unique craft making skills, you might also consider offering craft making workshops so local crafts makers can teach their skills to others who can then start their own crafts business. Such trainings would have to be more formal than the fun craft making events I mentioned above and you would have to pay these trainers for their expert time.

Public art is a whole different realm you might consider for your junked bike parts. If your local government is interested in public art and fun public furniture you might have a chance of contracting with them for your services. They would pay your organization to produce particular art objects and useful items to be placed on public property. For instance, your city government could hire your organization on contract to build one hundred bike parking racks out of bike frames to be placed throughout the city. Not only would this be an excellent income opportunity, but you could also request the inclusion of your organization's name, logo and website on each rack to add to your promotion and marketing efforts.

Bike Rentals and Government Contracts for Bicycle Service

Bike rentals and government contracts for bicycle service offer two more potential additions to your income generation.

Regarding bike rentals, be warned—they are not free money. I learned through my bike shop that bike rentals come with many unexpected costs. First, you have to set aside excellent bikes as your rentals. They cannot be worn out used bikes because bike renters are extremely hard on bikes. Also, you want your renters to enjoy their experience so they get their money's worth and tell their friends. The bikes will either have to be the very best of your refurbished bikes or new bikes you've manufactured at your center. Either way, you will be removing your best bikes from your sales floor, not only losing the sale, but placing these bikes in harm's way. Don't expect that you can rent your bikes and then sell them for the same price after their rental service. Some will have to be completely rebuilt, others might even be broken beyond repair. I was shocked countless times by the damage bike renters managed to do to my rental bikes.

This shows why you must have a very clear rental agreement that makes renters responsible for all losses and damage (find an example in Appendix D) *and* take an imprint of the renter's credit card before they leave your center. The agreement must state that they will be charged the full retail replacement price of the bike in case it is damaged beyond repair or not returned. It also must have the renter acknowledge that the bike was in good condition when they left your center and that any damage noted upon their return will be charged to the customer. Even with these protections in place, your staff who take the bikes back in are bound to miss extreme damage. If they miss the damage and check the bike in as in good shape, you cannot charge the customer for damages later. Staff at my shop missed countless broken parts and two broken frames. When a rental brings in twenty dollars, but results in the total loss of a bike that could have sold for two hundred dollars used, that's bad business.

This also shows that in order to provide well-tuned and safe bikes for people who rent them, your staff will have to do a mini tune up on each bike that is returned after being rented. They also must fully check and adjust each bike before it goes out for rent, including fitting the seat and handlebars to the rider, checking that the wheels are secure, airing the tires, and making necessary adjustments to brakes, hubs and derailleurs.

This takes a lot of staff time, which adds to the cost of each rental. Add to that the space the bikes take up as well as a possible increase in your insurance bills and bike rentals shouldn't look like discovered treasure anymore. Enter this venture with eyes wide open and low expectations.

Set your rental prices as high as your market will allow to give you the best chance of making a profit. Include an hourly rate, a half day rate, a full day rate and a weekly rate. Set that hourly rate to the max because it only takes a second for a renter to launch your bike off a cliff. They'll get a hilarious story to tell all their friends back home. You'll get a disastrous blow to your program if your employee misses that broken frame.

If you and your team do decide to venture into bike rentals you'll gain the experience and expectations necessary to scale up into servicing fleets of bicycles for your local government. This could even include expanding your rental fleet into city parks or at tourist destinations. You won't need to offer bike rentals at your center in order to compete for a government contract, but the similarities are noteworthy.

In recent years, a concept called bike share has spread to cities around the world. City governments contract with experienced bike share companies who set up multiple stations around the city with special bikes that can be checked out by passersby. These bikes are made with unique frames and parts to discourage theft. Sometimes they even have solid tires and added weight to make them even less attractive to thieves. Part of their frame structure includes a clamp system that connects it to the rack at any of the stations. The only way to release the bike is to either enter a membership number where a credit card is on file or swipe a credit card. The customer then releases the bike and is usually allowed to ride it for free for up to an hour before he or she must return it to any station around the city if they want to avoid being charged. The hourly rate is quite high after that in order to discourage people from keeping the bikes for long.

If your city is considering bringing in a bike share program, there might be some income potential for your center. Because these bike share programs are designed for tourists and affluent commuters, your organization should not attempt to contract for the full program, which would divert too much time and energy away from your core program goals. Leave that to the bike share experts. But, there are several sub-contract possibilities including repair of the bikes and even fabrication of some of the program's components. Start by discussing this with your city officials. If they are open to your center's involvement you could offer your program's services to the bike share company. If it's good timing, they could include your center in the final agreement with the city and set your center up for a long-term funding contract.

Variations of this sort of bicycle service contract could include bicycle manufacture, service and modification to fleets of bicycles provided to government employees. Sometimes a government agency will purchase bikes for their employees to use for short trips from the office during the day to avoid use of cars. Some post offices use bikes for their carriers in urban areas. Also bicycle police officers and paramedics are becoming more common in downtowns. Your center could contract with your city to be the service center for all of these bikes and even manufacture the bikes from the beginning.

Bike Education Contracts

You will need to include some bicycle riding education at your center simply to ensure that the clients you work with understand the basics involved in avoiding crashes. These basics include:

- Ride a bike that fits you.
- Keep your bike well tuned with proper air pressure, secure wheels and brakes that work well in all conditions.
- Follow all traffic laws.
- Ride in the road in the same direction as traffic or on a bikeway, not on the sidewalk.
- Ride predictably so that drivers will know your intentions.
- Ride at least three feet away from parked cars to avoid doors that open suddenly.
- Ride as far from the road edge as safety allows to ensure drivers see you; take the whole lane if there is no room for cars to pass safely and traffic speeds are low.
- Signal before you turn.
- Use lights at night.

If your city has a bike route map, offering these maps can be an excellent way to help folks ride safely. Sometimes people choose the busiest, most dangerous roads because they are not aware of safer ways to ride to their destinations. Even without a map, your staff can ask them where they often ride and then tell them about the safest routes to take.

Don't forget to offer driver education, too. In fact, the people behind the wheel of the two ton machines are the ones who need the most education about bicycles. Your staff and clients might have cars. Many of your retail customers will own a car. Make sure to include in all of your education materials and messages these important points for drivers:

- Bicyclists have the same rights to use the roads as car drivers.
- Give bicyclists lots of room because sometimes they have to stop suddenly or avoid hazards in the road you might not see; give at least three feet when passing.
- Look for bikes at intersections, slow down and don't expect them to signal a turn.
- Never drive or park in bike lanes.
- Never honk your horn behind a bicyclist, this only scares them and

could cause them to loose control of their bike.

- When you park on the side of a street, always look behind you for bicyclists before opening your door.

Train all your staff to offer these safety rules whenever they have a chance. Check with your local bicycle advocacy organization for materials or send away for copies of popular bike safety brochures to hand out. You can also make your own, adapted for your culture and clients.

Beyond this basic level of bike education, your organization will have the opportunity to expand it into an income generator. If your local government is motivated to educate cyclists to ride more safely, they might be open to contracting with your organization to offer classes. These classes could be held for adult riders at your center or in schools for children. Before you begin such a discussion, make sure your government officials are not trying to shift their responsibility away from providing safer streets for cyclists. Many times, lazy (or worse) government officials will blame bicycle crashes entirely on the bicyclists and point to bike education as the only means of improvement. Do not take on a bike education contract with your local government until you see proof of their commitment to *also* improve city streets for bicycling.

Bike Advocacy

Bike advocacy is a whole different game from Social Bike Business. I realize that Social Bike Business is in a way a sort of bike advocacy because it strikes at the barriers that keep disadvantaged people from choosing bicycling or benefiting from its career opportunities. But bike advocacy in its true form focuses an organization's energies on changing its community into a place where everyone wants to ride a bike. This takes enormous effort, focus and commitment. Years of negotiations with government officials can be cast aside in one election. Transportation funding that was won for a bicycle facility can be returned unused. To do a great job with bike advocacy, an organization must be completely focused on it, fighting for every street and policy improvement.

That doesn't mean that your center can't play an important role in the bicycle advocacy movement in your area. Start by connecting with existing bicycle advocacy organizations that serve your area. If there are no organizations that specialize in bicycle advocacy, look for organizations working for any transportation improvements that will serve pedestrians and bicyclists. Organizations that represent disabled people, fight for pedestrian rights, and advocate for public transportation are all potential allies. You can encourage them to include bicycle advocacy in their efforts and then offer to help.

If you still come up short on organizations who can lead the bicycle advocacy effort, check with your local government to learn what bicycle improvements are underway. Chances are there aren't any, but if there are, you need to know about them before getting involved in any bicycle advocacy effort.

Successful bicycle advocacy campaigns always start with a full assessment of the primary problem. It might be a needed roadway improvement or policy change. If no other organization is willing to take on this priority campaign, have a serious discussion with your board of directors as to whether it would be worth spending time and resources on such a campaign. If you and your team decide to go for it, try to keep the campaign as compact as possible and shoot for a win in a reasonable amount of time so you can get back to your good work at your center. Find some tips on One Street's website under Campaign Planning in the left menu and contact us anytime for assistance.

Because your center will become a destination for everyone interested in bicycling, it can become the place to find materials and updates on the latest bicycle advocacy happenings. Your staff can sign people up to get involved in campaigns (hopefully run by other organizations) and bring them up to date on the issues involved.

Another indirect form of bicycle advocacy is simply inspiring people to ride. Your center can contribute to your area's bicycle advocacy efforts through its events and social gatherings. Partner with other organizations in your area to bring people together for fun rides, bike parties and other events that inspire more people to try bicycling and take pride in riding.

Conclusion

I hope this book has inspired you and your team to take bold steps into the exciting realm of Social Bike Business. Look at it as your menu of possibilities and realize that you get to plan the whole festival embellishing the parts that most interest you and adding flavors from your unique culture to draw a crowd.

The Social Bike Business program is much more like assembling a festival than a linear process toward a rigid goal. You and your team will start wherever it makes sense to you, backtrack where needed, and then skip ahead when opportunities arise. As leaders, you have the power to control the speed and direction your program takes.

You and your team will need extreme focus and diligence in order to set in place the principles and systems that will result in your program providing bicycles and careers to people who need them the most. You will have to value the expertise of the impoverished people you aim to serve and create many ways to engage them in your program. But that is just the necessary framework of any Social Bike Business program. Only you and your team can bring your program to life by reshaping it to fit your culture and injecting the passion, enthusiasm and creativity that will inspire the people of your particular community.

Take that first step of discussing the program with people you respect in your community. Once your team forms and you're all ready to move ahead together, the dance can begin, set to your own music, but always moving toward that unshakable vision of defying poverty with bicycles.

If you ever think that One Street can help at any point in the development of your program, please don't hesitate to contact us. You can reach me directly at:

- +1-928-541-9841
- sue@onestreet.org
- Skype: sueknaup

For more information about One Street or to purchase more copies: www.onestreet.org

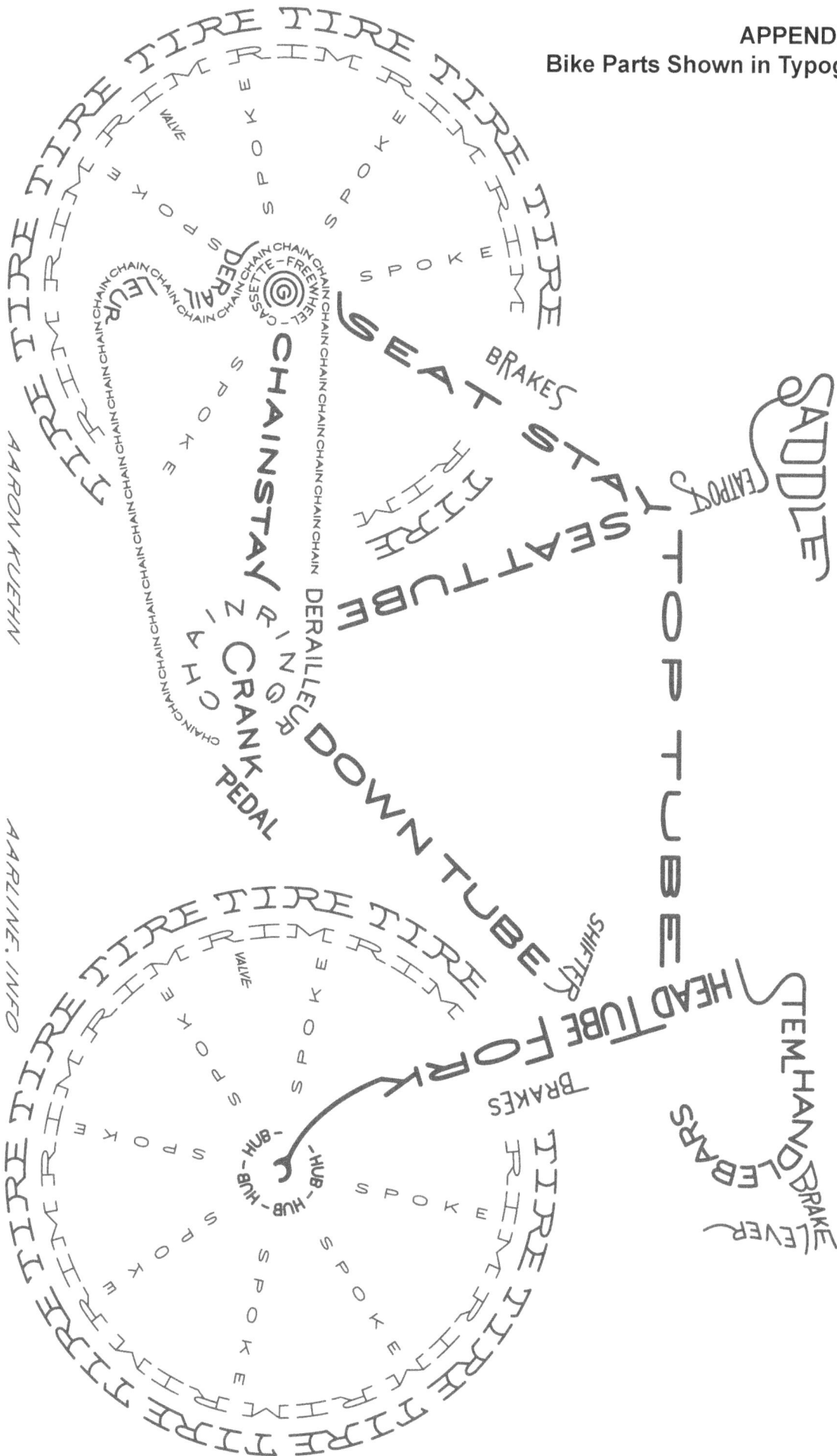

TIRE TIRE TIRE TIRE TIRE TIRE
RIM RIM
VALVE
SPOKE SPOKE SPOKE
CHAIN CHAIN CHAIN CHAIN CHAIN CHAIN CHAIN CHAIN CHAIN CHAIN CHAIN CHAIN CHAIN CHAIN CHAIN CHAIN CHAIN
DERAILLEUR
CASSETTE-FREEWHEEL
SPOKE
BRAKES
SADDLE
SEATPOST
SEAT STAY
RIM TIRE
SEATTUBE
CHAINSTAY
CHAINRING
CHAIN
CRANK
PEDAL
DOWN TUBE
TOP TUBE
SHIFTER
HEADTUBE FORK
BRAKES
STEM HANDLEBARS
BRAKE LEVER
TIRE TIRE TIRE TIRE
RIM RIM RIM
VALVE
SPOKE SPOKE
SPOKE
HUB-HUB-HUB-HUB
SPOKE SPOKE
SPOKE
TIRE RIM
TIRE TIRE TIRE TIRE RIM TIRE

AARON KUEHN

AARLINE.INFO

One Street's Bicycle Safety Checklist

Train your team to identify problems and inform riders respectfully about the problems they find. Train them to make easy repairs or convince riders to stop riding until repairs are made. Preventing someone from riding an unsafe bike is crash prevention. Numbers in the right column signify: **1 = Unsafe to ride, 2 = imminent bike damage, 3 = easy repair**

As observed from a distance:		**Pass**		**Fail**
Bike size	Rider's back and arms relaxed, not hunched or stretched, can straddle frame			1
Seat height	Legs extending fully and hips not rocking			3
Stem size	Frame is correct size, plus rider is not hunched or stretched			1
Squeaky	Chain is lubed and not rusty; especially important with coaster brake			2,3
Air pressure	Proper air pressure; dangerously low if tire flattens at ground			1,3
Quick release	Lever arches inward toward bike			1,3
Quick check (if allowed to examine bike, should take about ten minutes):		**Pass**		**Fail**
Frame and fork	Check from side and back for alignment, bends and dents; examine for cracks in paint or ripples in metal that reveal severe damage.			1
Quick releases securing wheels	Ensure closed (levers arching toward bike), then flick each with thumb; if they move at all, open, tighten nut, close, test again, until no movement.			1,3
Axle nuts	If wheels are held on with nuts, tighten all with proper wrench			1,3
Stem	Check insertion line; stand in front of bike, hold front wheel between legs, then twist handlebar back and forth; tighten with force if any movement;			1,3
Brakes	Levers must not touch grips when squeezed hard; smooth function and all brake parts and cables in good shape, bolts secure; test ride to ensure brakes stop bike; coaster brake should engage slowly, not lock.			1
Rims and spokes	Spin each wheel to check for rubbing and rim damage; squeeze spokes to check for balanced tension; if not balanced, wheel could collapse.			1,2
Hubs	Each wheel must turn at very slow speed to ensure hub is not over tight; grab tire and yank side to side to check for too loose.			2
Tires and air	Check tires for excessive wear or damage; fill to maximum air pressure noted on sidewall; ensure valve stem is straight otherwise could sheer off.			1,3
Headset	Squeeze front brake and rock bike to feel for loose; lift bike so front angles down, then push handlebar to check for too tight – should spin freely.			2
Bottom Bracket	Grab both crank arms and yank back and forth to test for loose; drop chain off and touch crank arm to check for too tight – should spin freely.			2
Pedals	Perpendicular to crank arms with no threads showing; spin smoothly.			2
Rear reflector	Install if missing; also recommend more reflectors and a headlight at night			3

As part of all repair jobs – all of the above, plus:
- [ ] ask owner to describe problems then investigate each;
- [ ] inform owner of needed repairs and costs;
- [ ] fine tune brakes, tighten all nuts and bolts, torque crank arm and stem bolts, tighten pedals;
- [ ] check derailleur limits to ensure no over shifting;
- [ ] test ride to check that bike is safe to ride and shifts and brakes properly; and
- [ ] adjust seat height to owner, ensure seat post is not over extended past min. insertion line.

One Street's
Bicycle Overhaul Checklist

Frame and Fork:
[ ] Frame checked for damage
[ ] Fork checked for bend or damage
[ ] Rear dropouts and derailleur hanger checked for alignment

Drive Train System:
[ ] Bottom bracket worn parts replaced
[ ] Bottom bracket greased including bearings, cups and frame shell
[ ] Bottom bracket fixed cup tightened to max
[ ] Bottom bracket adjusted and locknut tightened
[ ] Crank arms securely mounted and bolts torqued properly (350+ lbs)
[ ] Crank arm dust caps greased before installing
[ ] Chainring bolts tightened, none loose
[ ] Bent chainrings realigned
[ ] Pedals threads greased
[ ] Pedals securely mounted (no threads showing, as tight as possible)
[ ] Chain cleaned and checked for damaged links
[ ] Chain lubed and wiped down so no lubricant remains on outside
[ ] Chain inspected for wear and stretch
[ ] Chainline checked - chain to line up in middle of rear cogs when in middle chainring
[ ] Rear cogs cleaned and freehub checked for smooth action
[ ] Freewheel cleaned and rinsed
[ ] Freewheel inspected for wear
[ ] Freewheel oiled, threads greased and replaced, tightened with chain whip

Steering System:
[ ] Headset worn parts replaced, loose cups/races shimmed to prevent movement
[ ] Headset greased including bearings and cups
[ ] Headset adjusted and locknut tightened
[ ] Quill stem greased, height adjusted, aligned with front wheel
[ ] Stem binder bolt(s) greased, stem aligned with front wheel and bolts properly torqued
[ ] Handlebar inspected for damage
[ ] Handlebar aligned to curve up towards rider's shoulders, bolts greased and properly torqued

Wheel Systems:
[ ] Quick release (QR) hub axles adjusted so that they do not protrude past drop-outs
[ ] Front hub bearings greased and adjusted (QR hubs slightly loose), both locknuts tightened
[ ] Rear hub bearings greased and adjusted (QR hubs slightly loose), both locknuts tightened
[ ] Rims checked for damage and spokes protruding to puncture tube
[ ] Rim strips in place
[ ] Rims trued laterally and radially to .5mm tolerance or better
[ ] Tires checked for thorns, wear and damage, proper mounting, and inflation
[ ] Valve stems straight, presta valve ring tightened and caps installed
[ ] Wheels mounted in proper alignment, QR skewers tightly closed or axle nuts fully tightened

Brake System:
[ ] Rim surfaces cleaned and checked for damage
[ ] Cantilever brake studs greased and brake arms secured
[ ] Caliper brake adjusted for smooth action and no play, also centered
[ ] Brake pads sanded, replaced if too worn
[ ] Brake pads set parallel to rim to not rub tire, toed in to reduce squeal
[ ] Brake levers set so rider wrists are straight when reached
[ ] Brake lever pivots lubricated with light oil
[ ] Cables lubricated with light oil and replaced if worn
[ ] Housing cut for straight entry into levers and bosses, burrs removed, end caps on both ends
[ ] Cables stretched then adjusted so lever does not touch grip, adjusting barrels left screwed in
[ ] Cable ends capped

Shift Systems:
[ ] Rear derailleur removed and hanger checked for proper alignment
[ ] Rear derailleur inspected for damage and worn jockey wheels
[ ] Rear derailleur mounted securely
[ ] Rear derailleur pivots, cable adjusters, and jockey wheels lubricated with light oil
[ ] Rear derailleur limit screws set for shift to largest and smallest sprockets without over shift
[ ] Front derailleur checked for proper mounting height and rotation
[ ] Front derailleur checked for proper secure mounting
[ ] Front derailleur pivots lubricated
[ ] Front derailleur height adjusted to just clear largest chainring, aligned straight, bolt tightened
[ ] Front derailleur limit screws set to allow shift to large and small chainrings without over shift
[ ] Housing cut for straight entry into levers and bosses, burrs removed, end caps on both ends
[ ] Cables replaced if worn, lubricated with light oil and secured
[ ] Cables stretched by pulling down on them between housing
[ ] Cables adjusted to allow each derailleur to fully return to start point without cable slack
[ ] Shift levers secured so they face the rider's shoulders
[ ] Both derailleurs fine tuned using cable adjustment barrels

Bike Fit and Accessories:
[ ] Frame size correct for rider
[ ] Seat post checked for allowable minimum depth of insertion
[ ] Seat post greased and secure mounting checked
[ ] Seat checked for proper alignment and secure mounting
[ ] Seat and handlebar height/distance adjusted to rider
[ ] Accessories mounted securely with no interference with moving parts or safety hazards
[ ] Rear reflector installed
[ ] Rear rack installed
[ ] Lock attached to bike with key secure

Mechanic Test Ride:
[ ] Stem test – twist hard while standing in front of bike, front tire between legs
[ ] Brakes checked for stopping power and squeal
[ ] Bicycle checked for tracking and steering problems
[ ] Derailleurs checked for performance and over shift in both directions
[ ] Chain and freewheel cogs checked for skipping under load
[ ] Bicycle checked for unusual noises

(bike shop name)
(address)
(city, country, phone)

This form will serve as a **WAIVER** and/or **RELEASE OF LIABILITY** for (bike shop) and any individual or company acting as our rental agent.

RENTER'S NAME (must be 18 or older) _____

HOME ADDRESS: _____

CITY: _____ STATE: _____ ZIP: _____

LOCAL ADDRESS: _____

PH# _____ CELL# _____

1. I accept the equipment in its condition "as is." I have examined the equipment and determined that it is in good working order. While renting this equipment I will be responsible for its care and will return it in the same condition. I will pay for any damages or losses at the full RETAIL VALUE. **Initial_____**

2. I agree to HOLD HARMLESS and indemnify (bike shop), its owners, employees and rental agents for any loss or damage, including any that results from claims for personal injury or property damage related to the use of this equipment. **Initial_____**

3. I understand that all rented equipment remains the property of (bike shop) and agree to RETURN all equipment rented under this agreement in good condition by the agreed time to avoid confiscation of collateral and will pay any necessary repair or replacement costs as well as all late fees or collection charges, including attorney's fees. **Initial_____**

4. I understand that it is not possible to predict every situation which may arise while bicycling and therefore any safety equipment or safety features on the rented equipment are NO GUARANTEE for my safety. **Initial_____**

5. I hereby RELEASE (bike shop), its owners, employees, and rental agents from any and all liability for damage and injury to myself or to any other person or property resulting from negligence, installation, maintenance, selection, adjustment and use of this equipment, accepting myself the full responsibility for any and all such damage, injury or death which may result. **Initial_____**

6. This contract constitutes the entire rental agreement and there are no other agreements or understandings. **Initial_____**

LESSEE'S SIGNATURE _____ DATE_____

BICYCLE RENTED #_____ HELMET____ FLAT KIT____ PUMP_____ LOCK_____

DATE/TIME OUT__ _____ DATE/TIME IN_____

AMOUNT PAID (inc. accessories)_____

T his section is organized in two ways:

1) Full list alphabetized as RESOURCES to help you find them as referenced in this book,

2) Into their various categories:
   BIKE REPAIR & MANUFACTURING
   BOOKS
   BUSINESS PLANNING
   DATA
   FUNDING & MICRO LENDING
   SOCIAL BUSINESS
   U.S. GOVERNMENT

Thus, each resource is listed at least twice. Books are listed by their title, not author, because this is how they appear in this book.

RESOURCES:

- ACCION www.accion.org

- *The Bicycling Guide to Complete Bicycle Maintenance & Repair,* by Todd Downs

- *Bicycling Science,* by David Gordon Wilson

- *The Bicycle Wheel,* by Jobst Brandt

- City-Data: www.City-Data.com

- *Creating a World Without Poverty*, by Muhammad Yunus

- Eurobike www.eurobike-show.com

- European Small Business Alliance www.esba-europe.org

- European Twowheel Retailers' Association www.etra-eu.com

- The Foundation Center www.foundationcenter.org

- Grameen (find your local chapter)

- Homeboy Industries www.homeboyindustries.org

- Interbike www.interbike.com

- Kiva www.kiva.org

- *Made Possible By: Succeeding with Sponsorship*, by Patricia Martin

- National Bicycle Dealers Association www.nbda.com

- NESsT www.nesst.org

- One Street's website www.onestreet.org

- *The Paterek Manual for Bicycle Framebuilders*, by Tim Paterek

- *The Proteus Framebuilding Book: A Guide for the Novice Bicycle Framebuilder*, by Dr. Paul Proteus

- *The Rare Find: Spotting Exceptional Talent Before Everyone Else*, by George Anders

- Rickshaw Bank at Centre for Rural Development www.crdev.org/rb.asp

- Ride 4 a Woman www.ride4awoman.org

- *Small Time Operator: How to Start Your Own Business, Keep Your books, Pay Your Taxes, and Stay out of Trouble*, by Bernard B. Kamoroff, CPA

- Social Bike Business Budapest www.zofi.hu/projektek/socialbike

- Social Enterprise Toolbelt www.setoolbelt.org

- TechSoup www.techsoup.org

- U.S. Census Bureau www.census.gov

- U.S. Consumer Product Safety Commission (CPSC) www.cpsc.gov

- U.S. Federal Trade Commission www.ftc.gov

- U.S. IRS www.irs.gov

- U.S. IRS Business Structures web page www.irs.gov/businesses/small/article/0,,id=98359,00.html

- U.S. Securities and Exchange Commission www.sec.gov

- U.S. Small Business Administration www.sba.gov

- U.S. Small Business Administration's Business Plan Template http://web.sba.gov/busplantemplate/BizPlanStart.cfm

- U.S. Small Business Administration's microloan program www.sba.gov/content/microloan-program

- Welding overview www.gowelding.org

- World Bank's data site data.worldbank.org/

- World Health Organization (WHO) www.who.int/en

BIKE REPAIR & MANUFACTURING:

- *The Bicycling Guide to Complete Bicycle Maintenance & Repair*, by Todd Downs

- *Bicycling Science*, by David Gordon Wilson

- *The Bicycle Wheel*, by Jobst Brandt

- Eurobike www.eurobike-show.com

- Interbike www.interbike.com

- *The Paterek Manual for Bicycle Framebuilders*, by Tim Paterek

- *The Proteus Framebuilding Book: A Guide for the Novice Bicycle Framebuilder*, by Dr. Paul Proteus

- U.S. Consumer Product Safety Commission (CPSC) www.cpsc.gov

- Welding overview www.gowelding.org

BOOKS:

- *The Bicycling Guide to Complete Bicycle Maintenance & Repair*, by Todd Downs

- *Bicycling Science*, by David Gordon Wilson

- *The Bicycle Wheel*, by Jobst Brandt

- *Creating a World Without Poverty*, by Muhammad Yunus

- *Made Possible By: Succeeding with Sponsorship*, by Patricia Martin

- *The Paterek Manual for Bicycle Framebuilders*, by Tim Paterek

- *The Proteus Framebuilding Book: A Guide for the Novice Bicycle Framebuilder*, by Dr. Paul Proteus

- *The Rare Find: Spotting Exceptional Talent Before Everyone Else*, by George Anders

- *Small Time Operator: How to Start Your Own Business, Keep Your books, Pay Your Taxes, and Stay out of Trouble*, by Bernard B. Kamoroff, CPA

BUSINESS PLANNING:

- European Small Business Alliance www.esba-europe.org

- European Twowheel Retailers' Association www.etra-eu.com

- National Bicycle Dealers Association www.nbda.com

- NESsT www.nesst.org

- One Street's website www.onestreet.org

- *The Rare Find: Spotting Exceptional Talent Before Everyone Else*, by George Anders

- *Small Time Operator: How to Start Your Own Business, Keep Your books, Pay Your Taxes, and Stay out of Trouble*, by Bernard B. Kamoroff, CPA

- TechSoup www.techsoup.org

- U.S. IRS www.irs.gov

- U.S. IRS Business Structures web page www.irs.gov/businesses/small/article/0,,id=98359,00.html

- U.S. Small Business Administration www.sba.gov

- U.S. Small Business Administration's Business Plan Template http://web.sba.gov/busplantemplate/BizPlanStart.cfm

DATA:

- City-Data www.City-Data.com

- U.S. Census Bureau www.census.gov

- World Bank's data site data.worldbank.org/

- World Health Organization (WHO) www.who.int/en

FUNDING & MICRO LENDING:

- ACCION www.accion.org

- The Foundation Center www.foundationcenter.org

- Kiva www.kiva.org

- *Made Possible By: Succeeding with Sponsorship*, by Patricia Martin

- U.S. Federal Trade Commission www.ftc.gov

- U.S. Securities and Exchange Commission www.sec.gov

- U.S. Small Business Administration's microloan program www.sba.gov/content/microloan-program

SOCIAL BUSINESS:

- ACCION www.accion.org

- *Creating a World Without Poverty*, by Muhammad Yunus

- Grameen (find your local chapter)

- Homeboy Industries www.homeboyindustries.org

- Kiva www.kiva.org

- NESsT www.nesst.org

- One Street's website www.onestreet.org

- Rickshaw Bank at Centre for Rural Development www.crdev.org/rb.asp

- Ride 4 a Woman www.ride4awoman.org

- Social Bike Business Budapest www.zofi.hu/projektek/socialbike

- Social Enterprise Toolbelt www.setoolbelt.org

U.S. GOVERNMENT:

- U.S. Census Bureau www.census.gov

- U.S. Consumer Product Safety Commission (CPSC) www.cpsc.gov

- U.S. Federal Trade Commission www.ftc.gov

- U.S. IRS www.irs.gov

- U.S. IRS Business Structures web page www.irs.gov/businesses/small/article/0,,id=98359,00.html

- U.S. Securities and Exchange Commission www.sec.gov

- U.S. Small Business Administration www.sba.gov

- U.S. Small Business Administration's Business Plan Template
  http://web.sba.gov/busplantemplate/BizPlanStart.cfm

- U.S. Small Business Administration's microloan program www.sba.gov/content/microloan-program

ACKNOWLEDGEMENTS

This book would have been a mess without the selfless assistance of lots of wonderful helpers and proofreaders. Their many varied experiences and backgrounds gave each a different lens to read it through as they caught countless opportunities for improvement and additions of valuable information.

Michael Dummeyer and Taylor Kuyk-White were my first helpers as I sketched out the book concept. With the very first printout, Taylor's exquisite talent for editing steered me away from several grating passages, helping me smooth out the writing for our next batch of proof readers.

I can't express my appreciation enough for the five brave, early proofers who agreed to read the rough draft and offer their ideas for improvement.

Justin Hyatt, the founder of Social Bike Business Budapest and a long-time advocate for sensible transportation choices, offered his insights through his fresh experience of founding such a program.

Michael Linke, founder and Managing Director of Bicycling Empowerment Network Namibia, offered ideas from the knowledge he has gained through his eight years developing a similar program. He read the whole book on his phone while traveling back and forth between Namibia and Brazil!

James Moore, owner and business sage at Moore's Bike Shop in Mississippi nailed many spots where clarity on business practices was needed.

Dr. Paul Simpson, former board member and current advisor to the Centre Region Bicycle Coalition in Pennsylvania, offered his expert eye from his experience with several forms of organizations and bicycle programs.

Stuart Shell, board member for the Community Bike Project Omaha, offered real-time refinements to the text as he and his fellow leaders examine ways for their organization to take on Social Bike Business elements.

As these diligent proofreaders were hard at work, I was so pleased to receive passages and refinements from our partners and experts for particular sections of the book, including our three highlighted social businesses: Homeboy Industries, Rickshaw Bank and Ride 4 a Woman.

If you have read the book already you will have noticed many sections dependent on accounting expertise. As I typed out my request for help to One Street's wonderful CPA, Darlene Wood, I cringed at the number of pages I needed her to check. But she dug through them without a complaint and delivered many important refinements to ensure that new leaders can navigate around common accounting pitfalls.

Then Aaron Kuehn stunned me with his quick response and happy acceptance of my request to use his gorgeous bike parts typogram in Appendix A.

All but two of the book's photos were either taken by me or were purchased by One Street at istockphoto.com. One of the guest photos is from our partners at the 816 Collective in Missouri – the proud man lifting his bike in Chapter 2. The other is from our partners at Rickshaw Bank showing one of their manufacturing workshops in Chapter 3.

Finally, after I had made these important additions and changes and had dumped the whole book into the formatting software, I needed a few more pairs of expert eyes to look at the entire thing and offer improvements on every aspect. Johanna Hawley, my dear friend here in Prescott and long-time community activist, and my gallant husband, Jim Knaup, were my chosen final proofers. They both stepped up to the challenge with little more than a groan or two and delivered excellent refinements I never would have caught. Jim went at it from his business, organization and writing experience. Johanna checked and rechecked each passage for clarity. She also offered her design expertise for the book cover, adjusting the text layout to ensure the rider holds the spotlight.

This book attempts to capture the experiences of many One Street partners as well as people and organizations I have worked with since I was a teenager. There is no way I could acknowledge everyone who has contributed to its content. Also, because the process of creating this book spanned nearly two years, all One Street supporters deserve our great appreciation for making it possible.

But there is one supporter in particular who deliberately stepped up to ensure its successful completion. New Belgium Brewing Company has supported One Street's Social Bike Business program since our founding, including the publication of this manual in their last two grants. In fact, without their last grant we would not have had the funds to send it to final publication and print.

How can I say "THANK YOU!" loud enough and clear enough for each of you to understand how much I appreciate your help with this book? I've noted you here. I'll send you your copies. I'll give you a big hug the next time I see you. But still, that doesn't seem enough. All I can think of is to ask you to pick up this book, feel its weight, flip through its pages and recognize the role you played in bringing it to life. I hope that makes you smile, as it does me. Thank you!

Index